YOUR
SLIDES
SUCK!

Wow your audience with engaging, empowering and effective PowerPoint presentations

by

DAVID HENSON

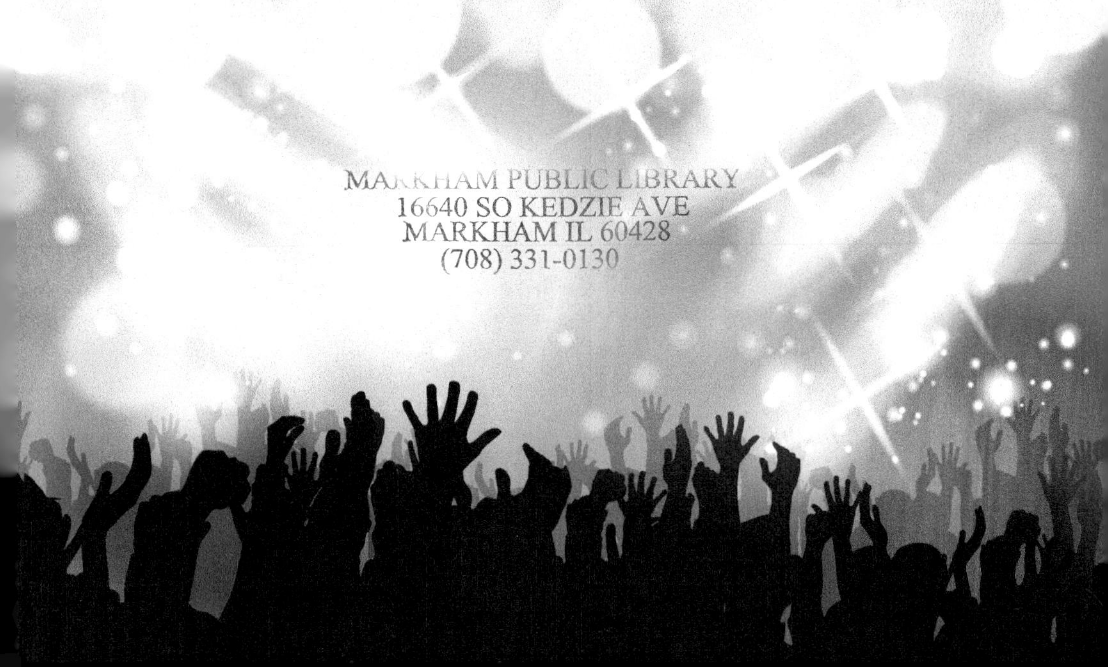

MARKHAM PUBLIC LIBRARY
16640 SO KEDZIE AVE
MARKHAM IL 60428
(708) 331-0130

©2017 David Henson

First Published in Great Britain 2017 by mPowr (Publishing) Limited

www.mpowrpublishing.com

The moral right of the author has been asserted.

All rights Reserved. No part of this publication may be reproduced, stored in a retrieval system, or transmitted, in any form or by any means without the prior written permission of the publisher, nor be circulated in any form of binding or cover other than that in which it is published and without similar condition being imposed on the subsequent purchaser.

A catalogue record for this book is available from the British Library

ISBN – 978-1-907282-78-2

Design and Illustrations by David Henson
mPowr Publishing 'Clumpy™' Logo by e-nimation.com
Clumpy™ and the Clumpy™ Logo are trademarks of mPowr Limited

mPowr Publishing Presents...

When you pick up a book by mPowr Publishing you are in for an adventure. Our passion is transformational content, ideas, stories, tools and strategies that empower lives, businesses and communities. You are not likely to get what you expect but you will always find what you need. We don't do bland, generic information. We celebrate the inner quirk, the outer quest and the joy of building legacies that last. Adventurers, Be Enchanted!

This book is dedicated to all those people who have ever given a poor slide presentation.

Without you, the book would not be possible (or necessary).

Contents

Introduction

Like me, I'm sure you've seen many bad presentations – the kind that make you want to gouge out your own eyes with a rusty spoon! (OK, maybe not quite that bad but you know what I mean.) And that's the reason I decided to write this book.

A poor slide presentation can affect your credibility and turn what was originally a professional speech into a disaster. Even good speakers use bad slides and, after the effort of drafting an excellent speech, it's a crying shame that it can all come unravelled by not giving enough thought to the visual aspects of your presentation.

This book will teach you how to give engaging slide presentations that will empower and, most importantly, are effective and help you achieve your desired result. The book is full of loads of examples to inspire you (as well as examples of what not to do).

It will help you to see your presentations in a different way and to put you in the shoes of the people who are going to sit through your talk and slides and see it through their eyes.

This is a practical book giving you things you can implement right away in your slide presentations. The first section deals with the question of whether you should be using slides; there are then three further sections: Setting up, Content and Putting on a Show.

In researching this book, I discovered that people have very strong opinions about slide presentations, especially PowerPoint. They get very agitated! But the tool you use is not important; don't be precious about it! There will be no argument here about whether PowerPoint is better than Keynote or vice versa or whether we should all be looking at Prezi or online forms of presentation. The best tool for the job is the one you're comfortable using and the one that can do the job for you. You would no more use a Formula 1 car to ferry a French stick and some Camembert around rural tracks in France than you would enter a 2CV into a high-octane F1 race. Pick the right tool for the task in hand and the one that you feel most at ease with.

For me that's usually PowerPoint and the examples in this book refer to PowerPoint. However, the principles apply to whatever presentation software you are using.

Because slides are often dynamic and animated there are examples within the book with links to some bonus content – online videos of slides to illustrate the points being made and video screencasts taking you through a number of tasks in PowerPoint. These screencasts will be using PowerPoint 2013; PowerPoint 2016 came out in 2015 (logically enough) and not everyone will have upgraded to this version.

There are also some links to download material you might find useful such as the PowerPoint template and line-up slides.

To access the bonus content, just go to slidebook.tv in your browser where you can register.

Introduction by David Henson
Online at slidebook.tv/media/001

The videos and screencasts will be highlighted in the book like this. When you have registered, take a look at the introduction at slidebook. tv/media/001.

There is also a resources section on the website at slidebook.tv/resources. This contains all of the useful links that are in the book.

There are a couple of things that this book is not about. It's not designed to make you a good speaker but I will talk a bit more about this in the first part of the book. It's also not intended to be a technical manual. There will only be some technical background where it's relevant. The screencasts are also a way of keeping the techy stuff separate from the main purpose of the book.

Unfortunately I can't wave a magic wand so that, as a member of the audience, you'll never have to sit through a horrendous slide presentation again. But, if you follow the advice in this book, at least *your* audiences won't have to go through the same thing. And, if everyone else's slides still suck, imagine the praise and admiration you'll get when yours stand head and shoulders above all the rest.

Section
ONE

Do you actually need slides?

So you're probably thinking, I've bought this book to learn about what makes a great slide presentation and the first section is suggesting that I might not even need slides!

Well, yes, seriously it is. Too often when people are asked to give a presentation, they immediately pull out their laptop or turn on their PC, open up PowerPoint and start typing away. But there are several factors to consider before you even get to that stage.

CHAPTER ONE

A SAMPLE
of RICE

Now you're probably wondering what the heck a sample of rice has got to with anything.

Well, SAMPLE and RICE are two acronyms that will help you to decide if you need to use slides in your presentation. SAMPLE establishes the parameters of your presentation – the six things you should consider before starting work on your speech or presentation, and RICE is a handy way of determining if a particular point you are making could be made better with the use of a slide or graphic.

So let's start with SAMPLE.

What are you talking about?

The first letter of SAMPLE is the S which stands for **Subject**.

The first thing you need to know is what you will be talking about. What is the subject of your speech? This should be the simplest part of the process because you probably already know. If you have been asked to give a presentation I would hope that the person asking you would have told you what you'll be speaking about!

It may be that you have been given a free hand to speak about whatever you want but before you can go any further in the process, you still need to know what you are going to be talking about.

Who are you talking to?

Then we come to the A, for **Audience**. It's important to know who you will be talking to; who is your audience?

Find out as much as you can about the people to whom you will be presenting. It may be a presentation to work colleagues you already know well. It may be to a roomful of complete strangers but who are these people? What's their background both personally and professionally?

Let's take an example. You're a health and fitness expert and you have been asked to give a presentation on how people can keep themselves fit and healthy, strangely enough! You know exactly what it takes to keep in shape, after all you're up at the crack of dawn jogging through the back streets, taking outdoor fitness classes with people of all shapes and sizes. But you know that your advice is going to be very different for different types of people. What would your approach be for the following audiences?

- ▶ Teenage schoolchildren

- ▶ New mums wanting to lose that baby bulge

- ▶ A professional sports team

- ▶ Over 70s

- ▶ Wounded war veterans

Ask as many questions as you can to find out more about your audience. If it was one of the above five groups for example, you might need to break it down even more. For a professional sports team:

- ▶ What sport?

- ▶ Male, female or mixed?

- ▶ What level?

If it's the Over 70s group then:

- ▶ Male, female or a mixed group?

- ▶ Are they already quite a fit group or are you talking to members of a group with a particular condition?

Put yourself in your audience's shoes. Imagine yourself sitting watching your presentation and ask the question: "What's in it for me?" What do you want the audience to get out of your presentation? How do you want them to change their behaviour? How do you want them to think or act after they've seen your presentation?

Get under the skin of your audience because until you know who you are going to be talking to, you're not ready to move on to the next step.

What's your takeaway?

Part three of SAMPLE is the all-important M for **Message**.

Once you know what you are talking about and who you are talking to, you can then decide what your message will be. You cannot decide on your message before you've covered the subject and the audience.

Telling your audience to run two miles a day to keep fit and healthy will be completely inappropriate for a group of over 70s who've all just been through hip replacement surgery.

Your message is the most important part of your presentation or speech.

What do you want people to take away after they have heard you speak? It may be one big thing or it may be two or three nuggets of information or an action that they can put into practice.

Your whole presentation should be crafted around this message. Start off by writing down the key message or messages that you want to get across and then you can work out what you need to say or show in order to convey the message to your audience.

Where are you presenting?

The P stands for **Place** – the venue or location where you will be presenting.

It might be in a small boardroom to a handful of people or a larger venue with maybe tens, hundreds or even thousands of people. The environment in which you are presenting will have an influence on how you are going to present.

Does the venue have audio-visual facilities for example? For our purposes, when it comes to presenting with slides, this is an important consideration.

There are so many different types of venue. I had to give a talk once in a cordoned-off area of a bar. The noise from other parts of the bar was quite distracting so I had to speak louder than usual and get as close to the audience as possible. After an hour of shouting, I was beginning to get quite hoarse. Luckily, being a bar, I was able to assuage my dry throat with a nice cold beer – just one during the talk and a couple more afterwards! (By the way, everyone else was drinking as well on that occasion. It wouldn't have been professional of course for me to have stood there quaffing ale-based comestibles otherwise.)

If it's a venue with which you are not familiar, try to find out as much as possible about it. If you can familiarise yourself with your speaking environment then you'll feel much more confident going into your speech. It might also have an influence on how you present your message.

How long is your presentation?

L is for **Length**. How long will your presentation be? Is it a quick ten minutes or are you going to be on stage for a few hours?

The time allowed for your presentation will determine what you are going to be able to say and how you will say it. If you are doing a short talk, don't try and shoehorn in too much content. Concentrate on one or two key points.

If you've got to talk for two or three hours then it might be a matter of taking a different approach when constructing your content, but make sure you do so in a way that adds interest or value. From the point of view of the audience, they'll want to know how things are going to pan out over that two or three hours. Give them a good idea of the timings and agenda so that they know how that time is going to be spent. If it's a long presentation then you'll want some kind of audience interaction or break-out sessions during the talk otherwise they are going to be noisily shifting in their seats if they just have to listen to you for that time, however good a speaker you are.

Executing your presentation

So with the first five letters of SAMPLE, you are now armed with all of the information you need to make an informed decision on how you will present and what you will say.

The E in SAMPLE stands for **Execution** – How you will deliver your speech. The questions are: how will you apply all of the information you have garnered so far and what application or media, if any, will you use to deliver your talk?

You know your **subject**, you know your **audience**, you know your **message**, you know your **place** and you know your **length**. Using these things, you know what you are going to say and you can confidently begin to write the speech and assemble the visuals if you need them.

Only now should you start to prepare your speech. With everything you now know, you can make a decision as to whether you think your presentation will benefit from the use of slides or any other visual medium, or indeed props.

If you feel that you are able to deliver a speech without any visual or physical accompaniment then that's what you should do; don't use slides for the sake of it.

And remember, the use of slides will not bolster a bad presentation. Never use slides as a crutch to prop yourself up.

Summarising the SAMPLE

So let's sum up what SAMPLE is all about so that the next time you are asked or decide to give a talk, you can quickly and easily work out what you are going to say and how you are going to say it.

Subject. What are you going to talk about?

Audience. Who are you talking to?

Message. What do you want your audience to take away?

Place. Where are you speaking?

Length. How long is your presentation?

Execution. How will you go about your speech and what media will you use to present your speech?

The choice *not* to use slides may be more obvious to you when you get to E than the alternative. If it's clear that you shouldn't then don't. If it's not clear then you may well find that the use of some visual support will be beneficial in your presentation and this will become clearer as you start to write your speech.

So how do you decide whether or not to use slides or not for a particular point you are making? This is where RICE comes in.

Time for some RICE (or what's the point of slides anyway?)

You may often have heard presentation material referred to as speaker support slides. Let's get away from that way of thinking and instead, focus on them as *audience* support slides. (Don't worry, I'm not going to turn that into an acronym although you might want to if it helps!)

Your slides are there to help your audience, not you. Never use slides as a crutch or an aide memoire

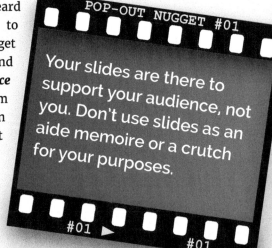

POP-OUT NUGGET #01

Your slides are there to support your audience, not you. Don't use slides as an aide memoire or a crutch for your purposes.

#01 ▶

#01

for your own purposes. The use of slides throughout a presentation may well help guide you through the speech, but that's not what they are for. They are there to make your speech more comprehensible to your audience and get your points across in the most powerful way.

Let's take a look at RICE and how it works. Take each point you are making in your presentation. Is it clear enough on its own or might it benefit from being accompanied by a slide? RICE stands for:

- ▶ Reinforce
- ▶ Illustrate
- ▶ Clarify
- ▶ Explain

Think about the point you are making:

- ▶ Would a slide help to **reinforce** that point in the audience's mind?
- ▶ Would an **illustration** of some kind help to increase the audience's grasp of your point?
- ▶ Would a slide help **clarify** the point you are making?
- ▶ Would the use of a slide **explain** what you are saying?

If the answer to any of these questions is yes, then you have a good candidate for firing up your laptop and designing the slide that is going to achieve one or more of these aims.

Let's take a few examples of where slides could be used to accomplish these goals.

What we'll do first is to outline the speech for the three examples. Don't turn the page over until you have read these. So here goes...

Example 1

"According to Dogs Trust, the UK's largest dog welfare charity, over 47,000 owners have abandoned their dogs in the past twelve months."

Example 2

"In the last 60 years the UK football transfer fee has increased massively. In the 1950s, the record fee paid was £65,000 increasing to £165,000 by the end of the 60s. At the end of the 1970s it had seen a nine-fold leap to £1,469,000. By contrast the 80s saw a relatively modest jump to £4.25 million by the end of the decade. In the era of the Premier League transfer fees continued to rise and at the end of the century the record stood at £22½ million. And then a decade later by 2010 it had again leapt, this time to £80 million."

Example 3

"The ecommerce payment process starts with the shopper entering their credit card details on your website. Your website then sends a request to the payment gateway, the company you have chosen to process your online payments. Based on the card number entered, the payment gateway requests a confirmation from the shopper's bank. The bank sends its response back to the payment gateway and the payment gateway in turn sends its response back to your website. Finally, your website shows the appropriate response to the shopper which will either be a successful payment or a failed payment. If it's a successful payment, the funds are then transferred from the shopper's bank to your merchant account."

Looking at the three examples, do you think that any of these might benefit from the use of slides? I think all three would (which is why I chose them of course). The next pages show examples of slides that could be used in each of the above three cases.

"According to Dogs Trust, the UK's largest dog welfare charity, over **47,000 owners have abandoned their dogs** in the past twelve months."

This slide appeals to the emotions of the audience. People can't resist a cute animal and juxtaposing this with information about the number of abandoned dogs helps add power to the message, **reinforcing** your point.

Slide 1. The abandoned dogs slide illustrates how an image can bring information to life.

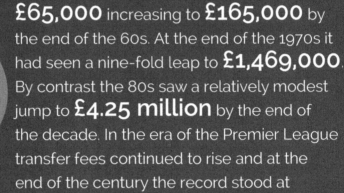

"In the last 60 years the UK football transfer fee has increased massively. In the 1950s, the record fee paid was **£65,000** increasing to **£165,000** by the end of the 60s. At the end of the 1970s it had seen a nine-fold leap to **£1,469,000**. By contrast the 80s saw a relatively modest jump to **£4.25 million** by the end of the decade. In the era of the Premier League transfer fees continued to rise and at the end of the century the record stood at **£22½ million**. And then a decade later by 2010 it had again leapt, this time to **£80 million**."

Hitting the audience with a bunch of figures is all well and good, but the comparison you are trying to make is not going to be clear in their mind if they are just hearing you talk. This sequence of slides (of which one is shown on the right) clearly **illustrates** the changes in the amounts over the decades and helps to clarify what you are saying. If you look at the build sequence online you'll also see how clever use of animation emphasises the difference between the bars as time goes by.

View online at slidebook.tv/media/002

Slide 2. When shown as a graph, the differences in football transfer fees over the decades becomes clearly visible.

"The ecommerce payment process starts with the **shopper** entering their credit card details on **your website**. Your website then sends a request to the **payment gateway**, the company you have chosen to process your online payments. Based on the card number entered, the payment gateway requests a confirmation from the **shopper's bank**. The bank sends its response back to the payment gateway and the payment gateway in turn sends its response back to your website. Finally, your website shows the appropriate response to the shopper which will either be a successful payment or a failed payment. If it's a successful payment, the funds are then transferred from the shopper's bank to your merchant account."

Explaining a complex process of any kind is going to be difficult without some form of visual backup. You may understand the process by reading the text from this speech snippet but if you are sitting in an audience listening to someone explain this, it may well go in one ear and out of the other.

The slide shown is the final slide in a sequence that helps to break down each part of the process as the speaker is describing it.

View online at slidebook.tv/media/003

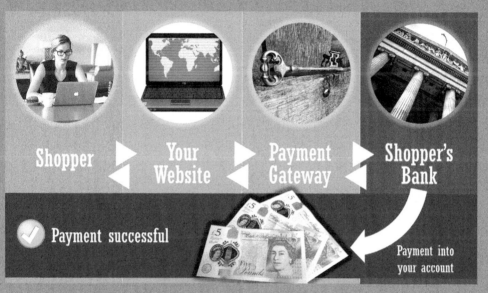

Shopper ► Your Website ► Payment Gateway ► Shopper's Bank

Payment successful

Payment into your account

Slide 3. A complex process can be clarified by using a build sequence of slides.

These three slides are examples of what might be used to help get the points across in the three speech snippets. By the way, don't forget to go to the URLs to see Slides 2 and 3. These slides both employ a build sequence which gradually reveals the information as the speech is unfolding. I'll talk more about the use of builds in chapter ten.

What if only part of your speech could benefit from the use of slides? My advice here is, don't be afraid to blank the screen. In PowerPoint you simply hit the B on your keyboard to blank the screen and hit it again to turn it back on. Your remote control clicker might also give you the option to blank the screen. Some people prefer to leave something on the screen in the background but that's entirely a matter of choice; you may feel that anything in the background will distract the audience away from your speech so that's where the B key comes in very handy.

POP-OUT NUGGET #02

Don't be afraid to blank the screen if you don't need slides for parts of your talk.

#02 ▶ #02

It's also important to bear in mind that using slides will straitjacket you into presenting exactly what's in the slide presentation. There's no room to veer off and go onto another subject. Slides will structure your presentation in a way that might be uncomfortable for some speakers, especially those who are more used to *going naked* (not literally of course!). I produced some slides for a top speaker where he forgot a small section of his talk. He moved onto the next slide and, when he saw it, realised that this was the bit he'd forgotten and he had to backtrack. If he'd not been using slides he could easily have missed

POP-OUT NUGGET #03

Bear in mind that slides will structure your presentation in a way that might be uncomfortable for some speakers.

#03 ▶ #03

that bit out and probably no-one would have noticed. So it's important to rehearse. Bear in mind that a slide presentation will dictate your talk and any mistakes in your speech may be highlighted by using slides.

RICE is not just for slides

When your points need to be Reinforced, Illustrated, Clarified or Explained there are various ways to achieve this; slides are not your only option.

Props

It may be that the point you are making can best be illustrated with the use of props. For example, I saw an osteopath explain to an audience about nerve impingement using a model spine. Talks about practical processes such as cooking, bike repair and craft work are pointless without demonstrating the action or process involved.

Stories

The other way of achieving the RICE aim is by telling stories. This takes more skill but it's something that many professional speakers use in order to enhance the points they are making.

An instance of where a story could have been used instead of a slide is in Slide 1. A good storyteller might have told the tale of a particular dog who had been abandoned, taking the listener from the depths of sadness at the plight of the wretched animal, through the ups and downs of its treatment and recovery, to the point where it is rehomed with a new family. They might make the point that many other dogs are not so lucky, finishing with the line: "Forty-seven thousand dogs were abandoned in the UK in the past twelve months."

So I'm not going to use slides! What next?

What if you've decided after going through the SAMPLE and RICE process that your speech doesn't need slides?

If you're confident about delivering it *naked* then go for it but what if you're not a confident public speaker? As I've already said, don't use slides or any other kind of visuals aids as a veil to cover up your own speaking imperfections. If you're not good at something (such as public speaking) then you've got four choices:

1	Don't do it
2	Do it badly
3	Get someone else to do it
4	Learn how to do it

If you've been asked to do a presentation then number 1 isn't a choice. Number 2 isn't either – a bad performance won't impress your audience or the organiser. If it's your boss in charge then your chances of promotion might well suffer a bit of a setback!

If you are in a position to delegate it then of course number 3 is an option, but do you really want someone else getting all the praise and attention?

The only sensible option is number 4. (This is the reason you've bought this book!)

When it comes to public speaking, if you want to learn to be a more confident speaker then visit your local Toastmasters club. Don't be put off by the name, it's got nothing to do with the kind of toastmaster who wears a red coat and officiates at ceremonies; no, it's a speakers' club where you can learn to become more confident talking in front of people, even if you start off as a gibbering wreck. It's done in a supportive and friendly environment and, as a Toastmaster myself, I can highly recommend it. For more information, and to find your nearest club, go to **www.toastmasters.org**.

Finally, before I move on to talk about slides, one of the best resources for watching great speeches is TED. TED is a non-profit organisation devoted to spreading ideas, usually in the form of short, powerful talks (eighteen minutes or less) and covering almost all topics — from science to business to global issues — in more than 100 languages. There are some really exceptional talks on TED and you'll see that some of them use slides or other visual aids and some don't. Go to www.ted.com to find out more.

So after the SAMPLE and RICE processes, you've come to the conclusion that you need to use slides for your presentation. So let's get going!

Section
TWO

Setting up

It's important to get the basics right and this section concentrates on how to set things up so that you have a strong basis for a great presentation.

You'll learn how to keep things simple (which makes it easier for you as well as much better for your audience) and you'll explore elements of design such as colours, fonts and layout.

Finally we'll cover how to create a template that will work for your presentation.

CHAPTER TWO

A Good Start

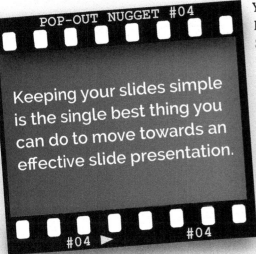

POP-OUT NUGGET #04

Keeping your slides simple is the single best thing you can do to move towards an effective slide presentation.

#04 ▶ #04

You've probably heard of the acronym: KISS. It stands for "Keep It Simple, Stupid". Whilst I agree with the sentiment of KISS, I would shrink from calling any of my readers stupid so I'm going to change it to "Keep It Short and Simple"; that's much friendlier. (And what with SAMPLE, RICE and now KISS, you're probably getting a bit fed up with acronyms, so I promise – no more acronyms or TLAs* for the rest of the book.)

Keeping your slides simple is the single best thing you can do to move towards an effective slide presentation.

Take a look at the slide below. What's wrong with it?

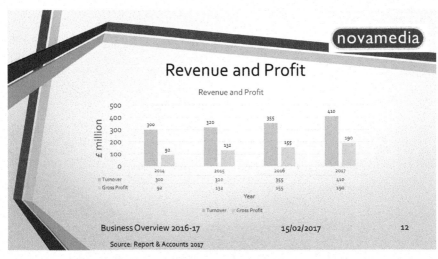

Slide 4. A bar graph – but what's wrong with it?

Well there are quite a few things wrong with it, but because we're talking about simplicity, you probably know the answer I'm looking for. The slide is too cluttered. There are superfluous elements on the slide that don't need to be there.

Date

Do you think that your audience don't know what the date is? Even if they don't, do you think that your slides should be their main source of information on this topic? No! I can think of no good reason why any slide in your presentation needs to show the date.

Slide number

Likewise, the slide number. What benefit is it to your audience to know that you are on slide 12? Is it slide 12 of 20 or slide 12 of 200? The slide number is unnecessary. It's also not going to be accurate in cases where you are using a build sequence. Take the example of the slide earlier showing the payment process. If you watched the animated version at slidebook.tv/media/003 you will have seen that the slide builds up in eight parts. So this is effectively eight slides but in PowerPoint it's only two, so if there were slide numbers on them, the number would only change once which makes the use of a slide number even less meaningful.

Presentation title

Why do some people insist on repeating the slide presentation title on each of their slides? The title should be on the title slide only. I would also assume that in most cases, the title of your presentation is going to be shown in a meeting agenda or conference booklet and also introduced by the MC of the meeting. It doesn't need to be on every slide.

Logo

I reckon that this one might take some more persuasion, but do you really need to remind everyone who you are or who your company is on every slide? As with the presentation title, your logo can be displayed on the title slide and at the end of your presentation. Your branding may well be included in the literature for the meeting and of course, you are going to be carrying lots of business cards to hand out to people who want to know more after your excellent talk and presentation and these will also have your logo or personal branding on them.

The logo on the slide is just one more thing that gets in the way of the information you are trying to convey.

Sources

If you are including information on your slides that needs to be accredited then you may want to put a source at the bottom of the slide. In general, unless you are legally bound to do so, don't put the source on your slide.

It is just adding to the clutter on your slide and so should be removed. You can, and probably should, put it on your handouts if they contain the same information.

Repeated items

There's never any reason to repeat any information on a slide. On this slide, the title is repeated. It's shown once as the slide title and then again as the title of the graph. We've also repeated the data. There's no need to have a data table under the graph if the data is shown above each of the bars.

Superfluous design elements

I'm going to be covering design in much more detail in chapter three but the KISS principle applies as much to the design and look of your slides as it does to the content. The slide is too fussy and the blue and grey bars on the left and at the top are unnecessary, just taking up space where the slide's content should be.

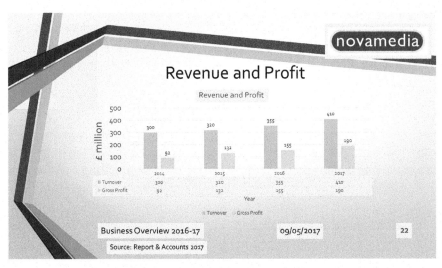

Slide 5. Everything highlighted on this slide is unnecessary.

So let's get rid of all of the superfluous stuff on the slide and see what we are left with.

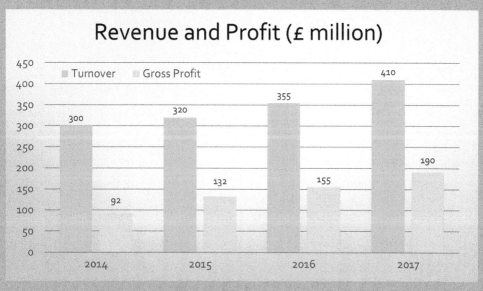

Slide 6. The same bar graph as Slide 4 but with all of the clutter removed.

Now we have a slide that contains only the information we want to get across in our talk. We've got rid of all of the unnecessary elements. This means that we've got more space for what's important – the content of the slide.

Remember – The only thing that should be on your slide is what is needed to reinforce, illustrate, clarify or explain what you are saying.

PowerPoint is terrible!

I can hear all the Mac and Keynote enthusiasts out there cheering fervently in agreement.

Often the reason there are so many superfluous elements on a slide is because PowerPoint encourages you to put them there. If you look at the slide master view in PowerPoint you'll see boxes for date, footer and slide number at the bottom. They are not shown on a slide by default – you have to insert them specifically – but the fact that they are there at all prompts many presenters to use them.

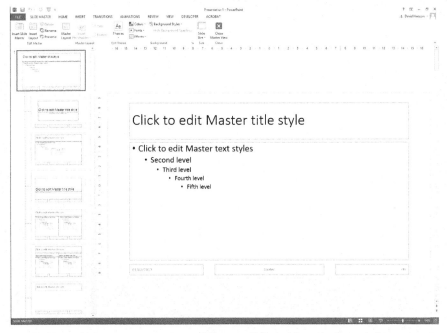

Fig 1: PowerPoint encourages you to fill your slides with superfluous elements like the date, the presentation title and the slide number. Don't be tempted!

You want to learn how to produce really effective and powerful slides. The good news is that means simplifying how you use tools like PowerPoint. When you go into the slide master view in PowerPoint you will see all of the different layouts on the left – titles, text, 2-column text, graphs and so on. *Go ahead and delete them all.* Yes that's right, *you don't need them.* You won't be able to delete the main slide master or first layout (i.e. the top two thumbnails in the slide master view) but delete the rest. Once you've removed all of the other master layouts, go into the main master and layout and delete everything on these two slides.

POP-OUT NUGGET #05

Delete all the masters in PowerPoint to give you full control over your slide presentation.

#05 ▶   #05

How to delete all master layouts in PowerPoint
Online at slidebook.tv/media/004

Your master layout should now look like Fig 2.

You have a blank canvas on which to build your slides and you are not encumbered by unnecessary complexity or clutter. Throughout this book I will continually urge you to keep things simple. That doesn't just mean the contents of your slides but also the way that you use your chosen software tool as shown with the PowerPoint masters. Keeping it simple not only makes the software so much easier and more enjoyable to use, it also means that you are going to create slides that are much more effective, eye-catching and engaging.

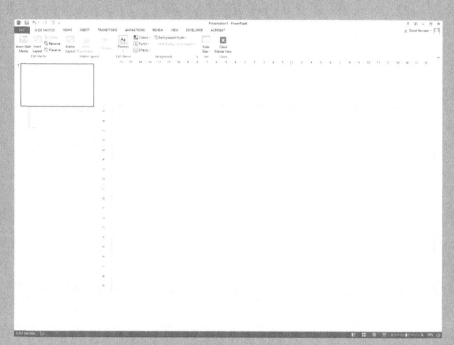

Fig 2: The PowerPoint slide master view with all of the master layouts deleted.

Help! What do I do next?

So you've just deleted all of the masters which PowerPoint helps you to use as a crutch to construct your slides. Why would you do that and where do we go from here? Because we have decided to keep our slides as simple as possible in order to make them punchy and effective, we will be adding everything to them manually. We can set up our own masters or templates (call them what you will) simply by creating great-looking slides and then duplicating these slides where necessary throughout the presentation.

You can match the type of slides you are going to use to the structure and content of your speech and it's an opportunity for you to be creative and project your personality.

CHAPTER THREE

Design It

The design of your slide deck is really important. It helps create a great first impression and boosts your credibility. It's the *wrapper* that holds the presentation and its contents together.

This chapter covers core aspects of design which contribute to the effectiveness of your presentation, giving it the wow factor.

POP-OUT NUGGET #06

The design of your slide deck is really important. It helps create a great first impression and boosts your credibility.

#06 ▶   #06

Slide size

The size and ratio of the page is not normally something that most presenters even give a thought to. They will start a new presentation in PowerPoint and just go with whatever is the default slide size. Since PowerPoint 2013, the default slide ratio has been 16:9; before that it was 4:3.

Slide at 4:3 ratio

Slide at 16:9 ratio

Fig 3. The difference between a slide ratio of 4:3 and 16:9.

16:9 is generally referred to as widescreen and is what our TVs tend to use. It feels much more modern than the squarer, squatter 4:3 slide size and is my preferred option.

If the screen you are going to be presenting on is set up for 4:3 then you might want to change the slide size but if you do, always do this *before* you start work on your presentation. Changing the size halfway through, or when you've finished work on your presentation, might throw up undesirable results. It will certainly mean you will have to go through all of your slides again individually, making changes so that they work in the new format.

How to change the slide size in PowerPoint
Online at slidebook.tv/media/005

Colour

What is colour?

Now here's a thing – colour doesn't exist! It's just that we (and other members of the animal kingdom) have evolved a useful pair of detectors on the front or sides of our faces that process the small part of the electromagnetic spectrum that we call light and that our brains then detect as different colours. Colour is just a survival mechanism.

"What has that got to do with my slides?" I hear you ask. Absolutely nothing, but I thought I'd temporarily digress into a philosophical talking point that you can bring up when you're next down the pub.

The human eye is capable of distinguishing about ten million different colours. We are trichromatic, meaning that we have three independent colour channels for conveying colour information. (Another interesting fact is that some animals such as butterflies and pigeons are thought to be pentachromatic, which means they have five separate colour channels and can detect about ten *billion* colours. They see the world in a much more colourful and exciting way than us.)

The three colour channels that the human eye uses are sensitive to red, green and blue light so it's no wonder that the colours on your computer have been designed to work in the same way.

If you look very closely at a computer screen you will see that each pixel is made up of different intensities of red, green and blue. Where all those intensities are zero, the pixel is black. Where they all are at their highest (a value of 255) the pixel is white.

So in total there are 256 values of each of the three colours (0 to 255) meaning that the total number of colours that your computer can show is 256 x 256 x 256. A whopping 16,777,216. This means your computer is capable of displaying more colours than your eye can detect!

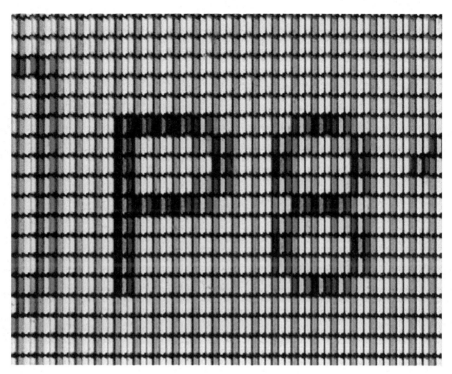

Fig 4. A close-up of a computer screen showing the red, green and blue elements of each pixel.

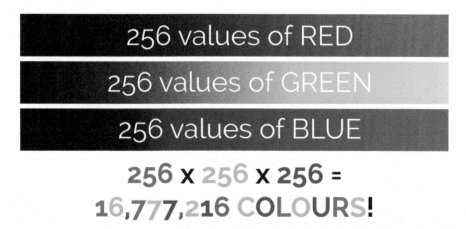

256 values of RED

256 values of GREEN

256 values of BLUE

256 x 256 x 256 = 16,777,216 COLOURS!

Fig 5. Your computer screen can show over sixteen million colours!

Using colour in your slides

So how do we choose which of those sixteen million-plus colours to use in our slide presentations?

What we don't do is go overboard and use as many colours as possible. Before starting on your slides it is useful to have an idea of the colours you want to use. Make up a colour palette of complementary colours that you can use throughout your presentation.

It's very easy to pick colour combinations that don't work. (Take heart! Nothing you do will ever be worse than the client who presented us with a disk of files to be imaged as 35mm slides where he'd used yellow text on a white background – yes honestly!)

POP-OUT NUGGET #07

Before starting on your slides, have an idea of the colours you want to use. Make up a colour palette of complementary colours that you can use throughout your presentation.

#07 ▶   #07

Slide 7: Yellow text on a white background – really?

Luckily there are some great tools that will help you to pick good colour combinations so that you can formulate your colour palette. One of the best is Adobe Color CC at color.adobe.com. (Don't try typing the word *colour* in English in the URL – it won't work!)

It allows you to create your own colour palettes by dragging handles on a colour wheel or you can simply use existing palettes that have been saved by other people. One of my favourite aspects of it is that you can create a palette from an uploaded image. This might help you to design a colour palette that captures the right mood. Take a look at the examples on the next two pages.

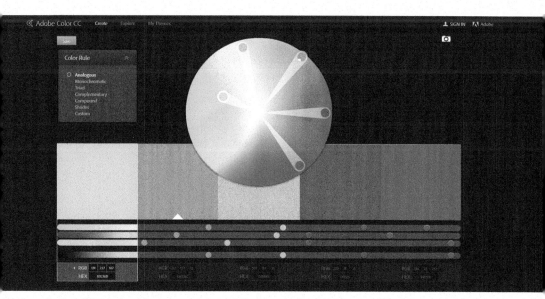

Fig 6. Adobe Color CC.

Fig 7. A corporate looking palette produced from colours in the urban image.

Fig 8. A natural looking palette produced from the uploaded image of the roses.

The first has a corporate feel to it whereas the second is more natural. It's no coincidence that the uploaded images convey the same mood as their palettes.

Of course, bad colour combinations not only affect your design, they might also affect the legibility of your slides. The same rules that apply to slides also apply to websites and there are some good web accessibility tools out there. You can use these to check if your slides are not only accessible but also legible, for example, contrastchecker.com.

POP-OUT NUGGET #08

Don't forget to include black and white in your colour palette.

#08 ► #08

When thinking about your colour palette, remember to include black and white. Black will give you the highest contrast against light colours and white will do the same against dark colours. Using only the colours from the natural palette will not give you sufficient legibility; introducing black and white into the palette will do the trick.

As I said right at the beginning of this section, don't go overboard with colours. A good thing about the Adobe Color application is that it suggests a palette of five colours which is probably about the right number, making seven when black and white are added.

In the next chapter you'll discover how you can use colour more functionally to help as signposts in your presentation.

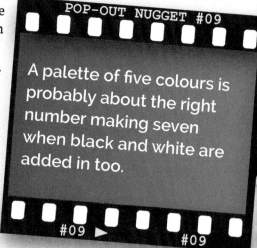

POP-OUT NUGGET #09

A palette of five colours is probably about the right number making seven when black and white are added in too.

#09 ► #09

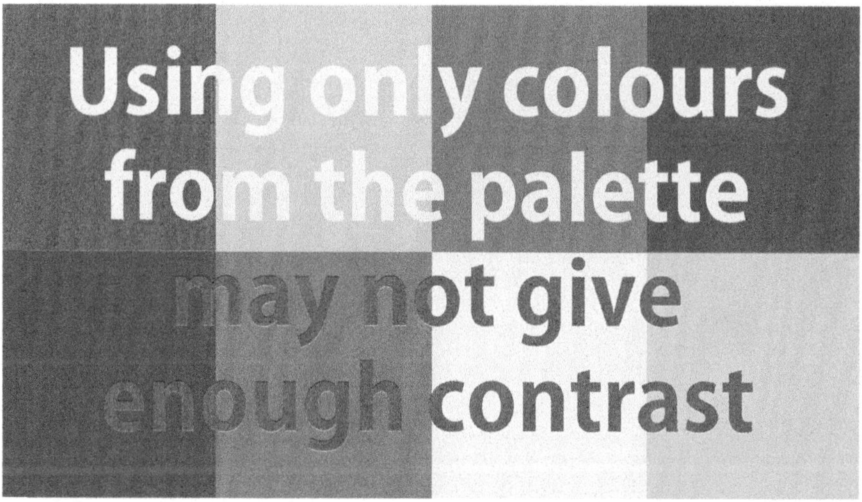

Using only colours from the palette may not give enough contrast

Introducing black and white to the colour palette will help lift the text

Fig 9. Remember to use black and white in your palette to help lift elements placed on the other colours.

Adding a colour palette to PowerPoint

Having chosen the colours you want to use in your palette, you then need to get them into PowerPoint. You can watch a video below explaining how to do this.

You'll need the RGB (Red, Green Blue) values of each of the colours. For white these are 255 – 255 – 255 and for black, 0 – 0 – 0. If you are using the Adobe Color application, the values for the five colours in the palette can be obtained beneath the large colour blocks.

Setting up the PowerPoint colour palette
Online at slidebook.tv/media/006

Fonts

With your slide page size and colour palette set up, the next thing to look at is the fonts you are going to use. (By the way, old school designers will argue about the difference between a font and a typeface. In the digital world, the two words are used interchangeably and it's the word *font* that tends be used in software applications, so that's what I'm sticking with!)

The font is really important. The tone of your presentation will be greatly influenced by your choice of font. I have two simple font rules that I live by and they are: (1) don't use boring, standard fonts and (2) *never* use Comic Sans.

Let's get the second one out of the way first. Comic Sans is a font designed in the 1990s and it's in the form of comic book lettering, as the name suggests. It is overused everywhere because, for some reason, people think it looks good. It doesn't! If you use Comic Sans in your presentation then, unless you are giving a slide talk to five-year-olds about a cartoon bear or a fluffy bunny, your credibility will go out of the window. Never, ever, ever use it – do I make myself clear? Excellent, rant over, time to calm down and move on.

POP-OUT NUGGET #10

The font is really important. The tone of your presentation will be greatly influenced by your choice of font.

#10 ▶ #10

POP-OUT NUGGET #11

Never, ever, use Comic Sans typeface!

#11 ▶ #11

Fig 10: The rule about the use of Comic Sans applies to any form of design, not just slides. This pub sign is the height of incongruity. Would you drink here?

Slides 8 and 9. Which of these speakers is the authority? The one on the left using Frutiger or the one on the right using Comic Sans? (Hint: it's a rhetorical question!)

Gone are the days when you only had a small choice of fonts such as Arial and Times New Roman. Despite being the mainstay of the digital media world for so many years, fonts such as these are now considered boring and distinctly old-fashioned. We have a much greater choice these days, which of course comes with dangers as well as benefits. Whilst I might have majored on Comic Sans with my little rant, there are many fonts which are almost as inappropriate when it comes to building an authoritative slide deck, either because of legibility issues or because of the tone of the font.

As with colours, don't go overboard; you should endeavour to keep the number of fonts you use in your presentation to just one or two. If you are using one, you can vary the weight of the font within the presentation to effectively give you two styles.

POP-OUT NUGGET #12

Endeavour to keep the number of fonts you use in your presentation to just one or two.

#12 ▶   #12

The four simple slides on the next two pages show examples of font usage and in three of the cases, two fonts have been combined on a slide to great effect.

Slide 10

Slide 11

Slides 10-13. These four simple slides show examples of font usage and in three of the cases, two fonts have been combined on a slide to great effect

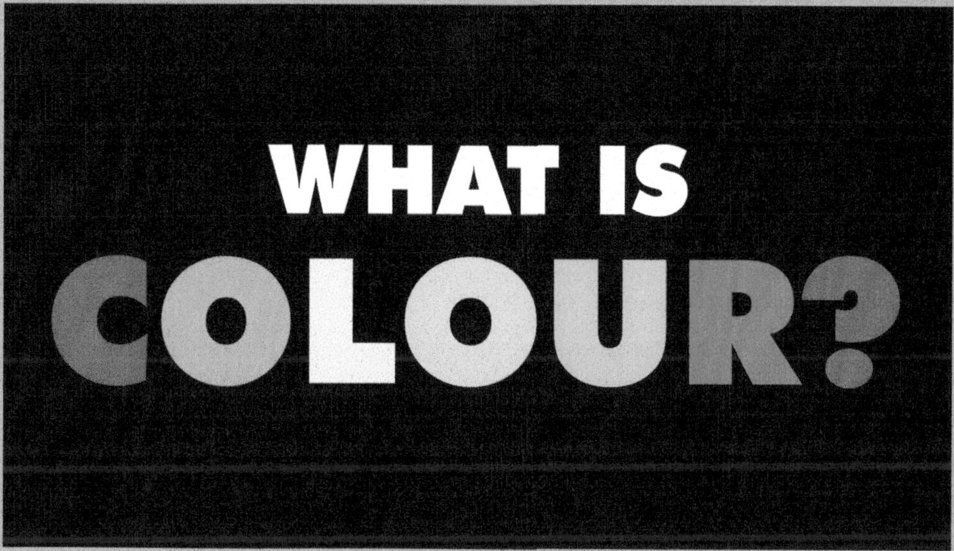

WHAT IS COLOUR?

Slide 12

An orange a day...

...keeps the doctor away

Slide 13

Font resources

Your PC or Mac will now come with a large number of built-in fonts and you should be able to find something that will fit the bill. But if you're stuck and need to find something different then there are lots of resources online that will help you in your search.

A couple that I would recommend are Google Fonts and Font Squirrel. To view and download Google Fonts just go to **www.google.com/fonts**. There are hundreds of open source fonts in the Google collection. You can easily download a font for use on your local PC or Mac.

Font Squirrel (**www.fontsquirrel.com**) also contains hundreds of fonts, most of which are free and easy to download with one click.

Embedding fonts

One issue with PowerPoint is that fonts aren't always portable from one PC to another. You might have put a lot of effort into selecting the right fonts only to find that, when you've handed the presentation over to the AV company or the conference organisers, it looks nothing like you intended.

The way round this is to make sure that the fonts you use are embedded in your PowerPoint presentation.

Better still, if you can, use your own laptop to make your presentation. Remember to check that the fonts are installed on your laptop if you are transferring a presentation from your desktop PC onto your laptop.

Embedding fonts in your PowerPoint presentation
Online at slidebook.tv/media/007

Declutter your background

Hang on, haven't we already done this bit? Well no, because what we are looking at now is the background of your slides, and not the content elements.

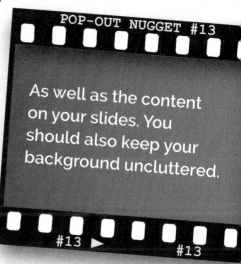

POP-OUT NUGGET #13

As well as the content on your slides. You should also keep your background uncluttered.

#13 ▶   #13

I'm not saying that you should only use a plain, coloured background, although there's nothing wrong with that. But try to avoid some of the designs that, again sadly, PowerPoint encourages you to use within its themes library. These are the designs that use graphics and other design elements that consume space on your slide that should be available for your all-important content. They are redundant and unnecessary.

Slide 14

Slide 15

Slide 16

Slide 17

You can see plenty of examples of slides in this book where the background has been decluttered and the design elements don't get in the way of the content.

Adding a background to a PowerPoint slide

To add a background to a PowerPoint slide, right-click in the slide and select *Format Background*. The *Format Background* panel will appear on the right. Here you can select from solid fill, gradient fill, picture or text fill and pattern fill. Pattern fill is best avoided. Try adding a few patterns to your background and you'll see why. You should also be careful if using picture or texture fill. It can work well but it can also produce a very distracting and cluttered background effect.

Select which kind of background you want and adjust the various settings to get the background exactly the way you want it.

Adding a background to a PowerPoint slide
Online at slidebook.tv/media/008

Be consistent

Finally when it comes to the design of your slides, make sure you are consistent.

The chosen colour palette should ensure that your colours are consistent throughout the presentation but don't be tempted to use them all as title colours on different slides. Be consistent.

We've already learned about fonts. Again you should endeavour to keep to the same font sizes and styles throughout your presentation if possible. Be consistent.

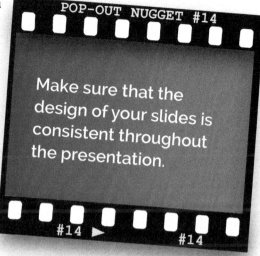

POP-OUT NUGGET #14

Make sure that the design of your slides is consistent throughout the presentation.

#14 ▶   #14

Lack of consistency in your design will confuse your audience and they may well lose their way and stop paying attention to what you are saying. Be consistent.

Consistency also applies to how items are placed on your slide. Employing a grid or using guides on a slide can be a good way of ensuring that various elements on your slides are positioned consistently.

How to add guides to a PowerPoint slide
Online at slidebook.tv/media/009

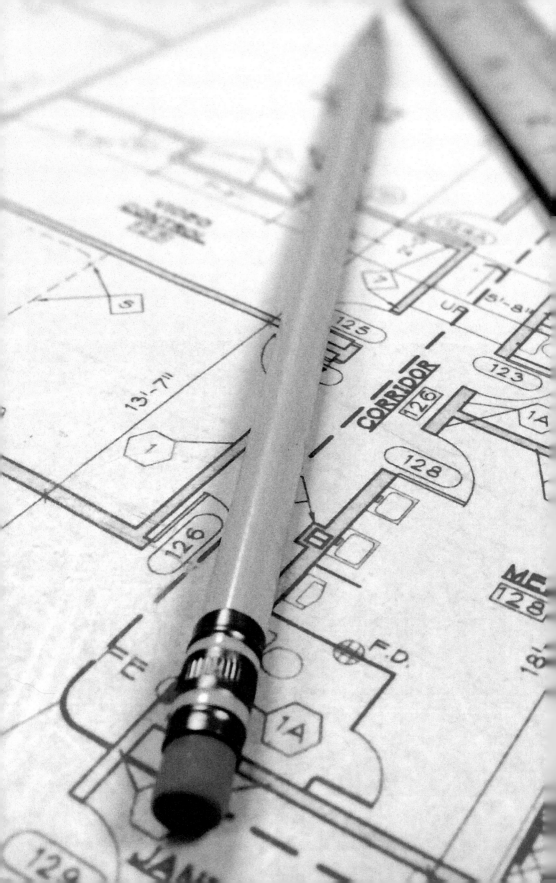

CHAPTER FOUR

From Design to Template

You're almost ready to start adding some content to your slides.

Before you do this let's take one more step: creating a template that we can use for our slides.

Why not use the PowerPoint masters?

POP-OUT NUGGET #15

Create your own slide template to give you complete control over the structure of your presentation.

#15 ▶

#15

In chapter two we deleted all of the PowerPoint masters and went back to a blank canvas. Why not use the PowerPoint masters?

There are several reasons why I recommend working without the PowerPoint masters:

▶ The masters encourage bad practice, especially when it comes to making your slides text-heavy.

▶ They are too rigid, forcing you into a straitjacket of uniformity.

▶ Your slides will look like everyone else's and, as you probably know if you've sat through any number of slide presentations, everyone else's slides suck!

▶ They'll randomly change the size and position of things without your permission.

So what makes your own template better?

▶ Your own template allows you to create exactly the right sort of slides you need for your presentation.

▶ It discourages heavy text use. You won't be going anywhere near a bullet point!

▶ It's easier to ensure the consistency that I was talking about in the last chapter.

Elements of a template

Consider the types of slides you want to use in your presentation. Here are some that you might like to consider:

- ▶ Title slide
- ▶ Section title slide
- ▶ Full picture slide
- ▶ Half picture / text slide
- ▶ Content slide with title

There may occasionally be others with different layouts that you might require for a particular presentation. The beauty of dumping masters and working with your own template is that you can easily create these.

Notice that I haven't added *bullet point slide* in the list above. We'll talk about bullets in more detail in the next chapter, but suffice to say at this point that one of my mantras is: the closer you are to zero bullet points, the better your presentation!

Producing the template

Producing a template that you can work with is really simple. One of the reasons it's simple is because that's one of our aims when constructing an effective slide presentation – simplicity. Furthermore, the template you design will also look very simple as you will see. All you want is something that lets you develop the type of slides you need.

If you followed the steps in chapter three, you already have your slide set up for size and your colour palette ready. You'll also know what fonts you are going to use. Your slide background is also set up. Mine is set up and ready to go as you can see on the next page.

Before you produce the template, it's a good idea to set up a slide like slide 18. It is useful for reference, as well as for copying and pasting bits for other parts of your template and presentation. It's a very simple thing to do – just create a slide with coloured boxes for your colour palette and a few text samples using your chosen fonts. The video link on the next page shows how to quickly do this.

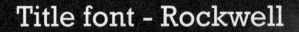

Slide 18. Reference slide for the hand-made template.

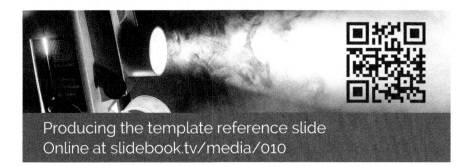

Producing the template reference slide
Online at slidebook.tv/media/010

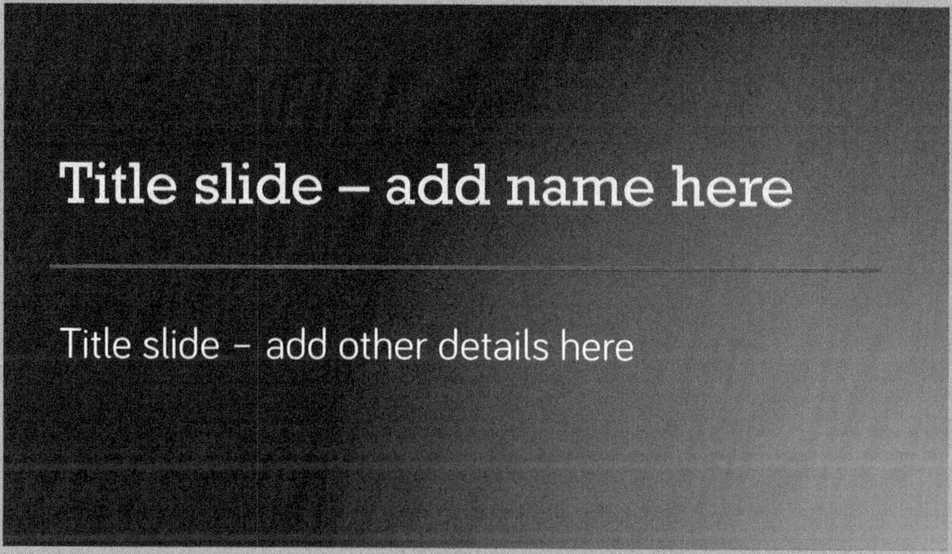

Slide 19. Template title slide.

Once you've got the reference slide prepared, the process of building your template is simple. The first thing to do is duplicate that slide. Then decide what type of slide you want to create and how it's going to look.

Let's say we want a main title slide. I've decided I want to use both fonts in my title slide and the colours will be the yellow from the palette for the main heading and white for the sub-heading plus the red from the palette for a dividing line. The result would look something like the above.

Easy, huh?

The next slide I want to produce is a section title slide. Before I do, I want to talk about signposting your presentation.

Giving your presentation a clear structure is important. It lets your audience know where they are in the presentation. For example, you may start by telling your audience that you'll be talking about three things in your presentation and show them a slide which acts as your agenda. Then, within your slide deck you should have section title slides which are clearly differentiated from the rest of the slides. These let the audience know when you move from one subject to the next. (It's a bit like this book being broken down into chapters with a contents page at the beginning and prominent chapter headings so that the reader knows where they are in the book.)

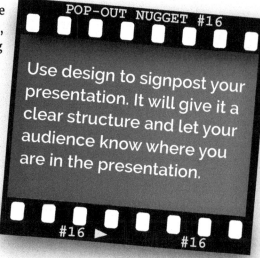

POP-OUT NUGGET #16

Use design to signpost your presentation. It will give it a clear structure and let your audience know where you are in the presentation.

#16 ▶   #16

So my section title slide is actually two slides with the same look and feel, one for the agenda or contents and one for the section titles themselves. What I'm going to do is to use one of the other colours in my colour palette as the background for the section title slides so that they are clearly differentiated from the main body of the presentation and we end up with something like the slides opposite.

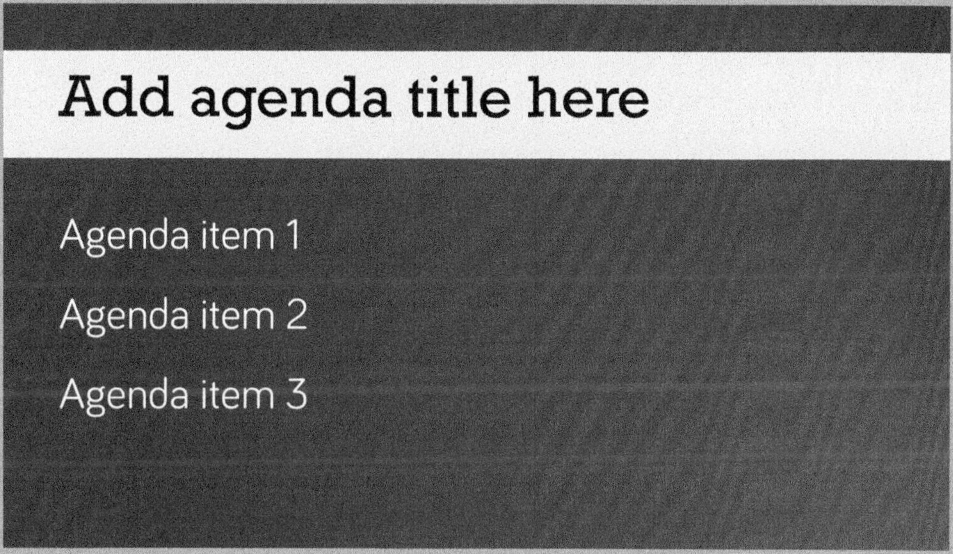

Add agenda title here

Agenda item 1

Agenda item 2

Agenda item 3

Slide 20. Template agenda slide.

Add section title here

Slide 21. Template section title slide.

POP-OUT NUGGET #17

Make sure that the longest title you want to use fits on the slide first before producing the slides with a shorter title

#17 ▶   #17

One final word on your section title slides (this applies to other slides that share similar design styles as well). Make sure that the longest title you want to use fits on the slide before producing the slides with a shorter title. If you've got one title that is much longer than the others then that might be more of an issue, but of course there's no reason why a title cannot go onto a second line.

The next template slide we want is the full picture layout. There are a few key points to remember when making this slide.

Firstly, never stretch a picture in one axis to make it fit full-frame on a slide (or on any part of the slide). If the picture isn't the same aspect ratio as your slide then you have two options. The first is to fill the frame as much as possible with the picture. If you do so then it's probably best to leave a bit of the background all around the slide. The better option is to crop the picture so that it fills the frame.

POP-OUT NUGGET #18

Don't stretch pictures in one axis to make them fit on your slides. The better option is to crop the picture so that it fills the frame.

#18 ▶   #18

How to crop pictures in PowerPoint
Online at slidebook.tv/media/011

Fig 11: Don't stretch pictures in one axis. It's OK to put a picture on the background but even better to crop it so that it fills the frame.

If you're filling the slide with a picture then you don't really need a template slide for this as you can just add pictures to the presentation as and when you are working on it. However another option that you might want to consider is overlaying text on a full-frame image. If there's not a dark or light enough area to overlay the text on the image then there are two alternative options.

The first way is to add a glow around the text so that it stands out from the image. If your text is white then you can use a black glow or sample a dark colour from the background image using PowerPoint's eyedropper tool. The other option is to use light text in a black or dark-coloured box that is semi-transparent or alternatively dark text in a white or light-coloured box that is semi-transparent. Whichever way you decide to do it, stick to that same method throughout the presentation.

Slide 22

Slide 23

Slide 24

Slide 25

Slides 22–25: Four ways to overlay text on a full-frame image.

How to produce the creative title slides
Online at slidebook.tv/media/012

Let's create our full-frame image template slide and set the text on top of the image. The image I have chosen for my template has quite a dark background anyway but I have sampled the darker part of the sky to add as a glow around the text to lift it from the image.

Slide 26. Template full-picture slide.

Slide 27. Template half-picture slide.

The way to design the half-picture / half-text template slide is to bring a picture into one half of the slide and add your text in the other half. For the purposes of this template I have created a very simple example, but I'll be going into more detail about images and how to use them in chapter six.

The final slide for our template is a content slide with title. Again, I'm going to use my two fonts, one for the title of the slide and the other for the content. The result is a very simple slide which is sufficient for our needs. It can be duplicated to easily produce slides of this type.

Add title here

Add body text here

Add body text here

Add body text here

Add body text here

Slide 28. Template content slide.

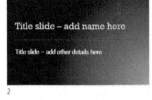
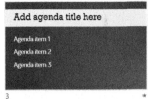

Our completed template is a slide presentation containing seven slides that are ready to be copied, as required, to build our slide presentation. Finally you are ready to start adding the all-important content to your slides.

This template is available for you to download for your own use at **slidebook.tv/media/014** along with some brief notes below some of the slides.

The whole template creation process
Online at slidebook.tv/media/013

Section
THREE

Content

So now we come to the content of your slides – what you're actually going to be showing to your audience to get your message across. In this section of the book we have chapters dealing with text, images, presenting data and video. It's all rounded off with a case study in which a typical poorly-produced slide is turned into something much more appealing and effective.

CHAPTER FIVE

Text

The first aspect of your slides' content that I want to address is text. As we've already established and as you will no doubt know if you've ever sat through a slide presentation, the ubiquitous bullet slide is the mainstay of many a slide show. Because slide programs encourage you to lay out slides in this way, people are duped into falling at the first hurdle, ploughing ahead with a series of boring, ineffective slides that are going to do nothing to communicate with and engage their audience.

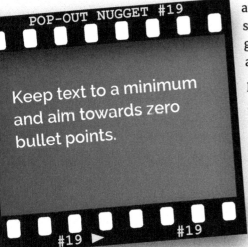

POP-OUT NUGGET #19

Keep text to a minimum and aim towards zero bullet points.

#19 ▶   #19

How many times have you heard a sentence such as "Ooh, I'm really looking forward to John's slide presentation this afternoon"? Probably never... am I right? But imagine people saying that about your slide presentation. Just replace the name *John* with your name (unless your name is John of course). That's what we're aiming for. Once you've delivered a stunning and engaging slide presentation, people are going to look forward to your next one knowing that it is going to deliver value and keep them absorbed.

The two simple rules with text content on your slides are:

▶   Keep text to a minimum

▶   Aim towards zero bullet points

What is the problem with text on a slide?

When you use slides with bullet points, what happens is that your audience switches between listening to you and reading what's on the screen. For the audience it is cognitively exhausting and it also means that, while they are reading your slides, they are not paying attention to what you are saying.

Using bullet points also has an effect on you as the presenter. If you use bullet points you become bullet points! What I mean by that is that, if your slides are dull and uninteresting, it's likely

POP-OUT NUGGET #20

If you use bullet points you become bullet points!

#20 ▶   #20

that will have an effect on you as a speaker and make you dull and uninteresting too.

The biggest no-no (which to my mind should really go without saying) is that you should *never, ever read from your slides*. If you're doing that then it either means that you don't need slides in the first place or that you don't need to be there. You might as well stick the slides up on the screen on a timer and let the audience read for themselves! Remember your audience came to listen and learn, to be motivated, inspired or entertained and not to read. If you want them to read something, provide them with a useful handout after the presentation.

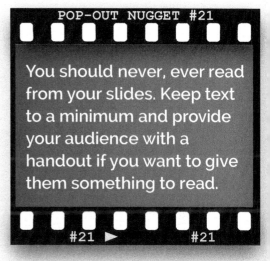

POP-OUT NUGGET #21

You should never, ever read from your slides. Keep text to a minimum and provide your audience with a handout if you want to give them something to read.

#21 ▶   #21

Unless you are running an interactive classroom style presentation, also remember that your audience didn't come to write. Tell them that they don't have to make notes because everything you are saying will be summed up in a handout which will be made available after your presentation. They can then concentrate their full attention on what you are saying for the duration of your presentation.

Bullet points

I have said that your aim should be towards zero bullet points. That doesn't mean that you should never use bullet points but that you should aim to keep them to a minimum. Aim to produce text points in a more creative way. The standard bullet (●) just screams *boring* and there's really no reason to use any symbol next to your text.

Let's take a look at a couple of examples.

> ## The Benefits of Lavender
>
> • It helps to eliminate nervous tension and anxiety
>
> • It can act as a pain reliever
>
> • It has disinfectant properties that help to clean the scalp and skin and keep them healthy
>
> • It can help to enhance blood circulation
>
> • It is able to treat respiratory problems and aid breathing

Slide 29. A typical bullet point slide.

The image above shows a typical bullet slide. The presenter will talk their way through each point. More often than not, all of the points will be on the screen at the same time, which probably means that the audience is way ahead of the speaker and reading the last bullet point while the speaker is still on the second or third.

The Benefits
of Lavender

Eliminates nerves

Relieves pain

Disinfects scalp and skin

Enhances blood circulation

Treats respiratory problems

Slide 30. A big improvement on the bullet point slide.

Now compare it with the slide above. It has a large picture of lavender on the slide; don't you feel relaxed already? On the right are the same five points but cut right down. On the first slide there were 48 words excluding the title and on the second just 14. The speaker will take each point in turn and the points should show one at a time on the slide so that the audience isn't trying to skip ahead. The text on the slide is enough to get the point across and the speaker can easily talk around each of the points without having to read off the screen.

The second example is a similar slide to the first lavender slide. At least this time the speaker has popped a picture of the camera they are talking about on the slide although it's much too small to be of any real value.

Camera Features

- It contains a large bright display that can easily be seen in full sunlight
- Multiple exposure modes that gives you full control of how you want to shoot
- The camera has an ergonomic design that feels more comfortable to hold
- 7 frames per second burst speed allows you to capture all the action
- 4K video at the flick of a switch allowing you to swap between still and movie modes

Slide 31. Another typical bullet point slide.

This slide could be improved by designing a series of slides each focusing on one point and showing an image of the camera controls or features to reinforce and illustrate what the speaker is talking about. The five slides on the right show this.

Again we have cut right down on the text because it's the speaker's job to do the talking and to add the *meat on the bones* of the points shown on the slide. The bullet point slide contained 70 words and the five slides on the right in total contain just 22 words.

You can see good examples of this sort of thing when you watch the news on TV. They will occasionally throw up a graphic on screen with a few text points but these will be concise and the news reader will be talking about them in more detail.

Slide 32

Slide 33

Slide 34

Slide 35

Slide 36

Slides 32–36: How to improve on the camera bullet point slide with a series of illustrative slides.

Slides vs. handouts

How many times have you heard a presenter say "I've printed these slides as a handout which you can take away and read after the presentation"?

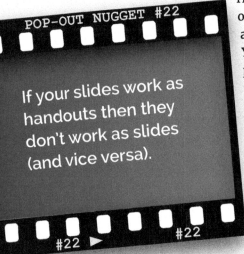

POP-OUT NUGGET #22

If your slides work as handouts then they don't work as slides (and vice versa).

#22 ▶ #22

Here's a really important golden rule and one that you should always remember and apply when producing a slide presentation: Your slides are only there for the presentation you are giving. If your slides work as handouts then they don't work as slides (and vice versa).

When you assemble your slide deck, don't think about what the audience will take away afterwards. Design the slides purely for the presentation you are giving so that they work for the ten, twenty, thirty or more minutes that you are standing up in front of your audience. Your slides are ephemeral, simply there to help you deliver a speech that keeps your audience captivated and makes them easy to remember afterwards.

If you are going to give the audience something to take away then create the handout completely separately from your presentation. Produce it so that it works as a handout and delivers value to your audience *after* the presentation. It means that you will have to do more work, but it will be worth it as you will end up with a presentation that wows your audience and a document that will help keep them informed after the event.

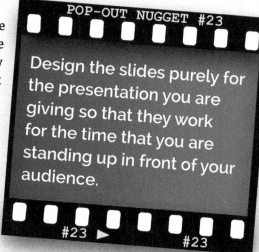

POP-OUT NUGGET #23

Design the slides purely for the presentation you are giving so that they work for the time that you are standing up in front of your audience.

#23 ▶ #23

One small final point about handouts. You should always make these available *after* your presentation. The handout will contain a lot of the information that you are going to be imparting in your speech and if you give it to the audience before you speak, they'll probably start reading it, detracting from the effect of your presentation.

Camera Features

Large bright display

The camera has a better and brighter OLED optical viewfinder display. This enables the viewfinder to be used even in bright sunshine.

Multiple exposure modes

Manual, aperture priority, shutter priority and full automatic modes enable you to take full control over the exposure of your shots.

Ergonomic design

Designed to be comfortable to use and hold for long periods of time, the camera will feel natural in the hands of the user for hours on end.

7 frames per second burst speed

So you don't miss any of the action, the camera will shoot singly, at 4 frames per second or up to 7 frames per second all in the highest raw mode.

4K video at the flick of a switch

A DSLR for videographers as well as photographers, full HD and 4K video can be shot simply by flicking a switch on the back of the camera.

Fig 13. The handout produced to accompany the camera slides.

Turning the camera slides into a handout might look something like the above.

POP-OUT NUGGET #24

Create the handout completely separately from your presentation and produce it so that it works as a handout and delivers value to your audience after the presentation.

#24 ▶   #24

The handout is where you can write all the text you need because your delegates will take it away and will be able to read it at their leisure. You can also see from the camera handout and from the preceding set of slides why the original camera bullet point slide was so wrong and that's because it neither worked as a slide nor as a handout.

Other points about text

Don't use text that is too small. Bearing in mind that you are keeping text to a minimum anyway, this should never be an issue. As a presenter, never use the following phrase in your speech: "I hope that people at the back can read this slide." Make sure they can!

Don't use your presentation as a teleprompter. If you have to use notes, use them in the traditional way and put them on the lectern.

Although you won't be using long sentences, it's still important to get your spelling and grammar right. People will be distracted by a typo or even worse by the misuse of apostrophe's. (Yes I know!)

Avoid buzzwords or management speak unless *everyone* in the audience understands them. Use of jargon will alienate your audience.

POP-OUT NUGGET #25

Use text that is readable at the back of the room.

#25 ▶ #25

POP-OUT NUGGET #26

It's still important to get your spelling and grammar right.

#26 ▶ #26

POP-OUT NUGGET #27

Avoid buzzwords or management speak unless everyone in the audience understands them.

#27 ▶ #27

CHAPTER SIX

Images

We are all more visually sophisticated than we used to be. We're surrounded by images all the time, on our smartphones, high-definition TVs, tablets, PCs or in print.

The old saying goes that *a picture paints a thousand words*. Very often it's true. Think about when you are watching the news. Images or film from around the world's trouble spots convey the story far more effectively than the voice of the newscaster can hope to do. And it will be the same with your slides. As I said before, if you are a great speaker or storyteller, it may be that you can get across the emotion of what you are driving at without the use of slides and of course, you'll remember RICE – slides should be used to reinforce, illustrate, clarify or explain a point you are trying to make.

POP-OUT NUGGET #28

The right image used in the right way at the right time is going to have a more profound effect on the viewer than just text.

#28 ▶   #28

When should you use images in a slide presentation? My simple answer to that would be: all the time! The right image used in the right way at the right time is going to have a more profound effect on the viewer than just text.

This chapter goes through everything you need to know about using images in your slide presentation.

A brief overview of image types and resolution

Firstly I want to talk about the different types of image files and then get an overview of image resolution. You can bring an image into a slide presentation without knowing any of this, but I think it's useful to know it as it will help you optimise your presentation.

There are various image formats, but the three that you are most likely to come across are JPEG (or JPG), PNG and GIF.

JPEG

If you are downloading photos from a stock library then these are most likely to be in JPEG format. The same applies to pictures you might take on a digital camera. JPEG will be your best choice if you are bringing photos into your slide presentation.

JPEG uses compression to keep the file size small and this is especially important if your slide deck contains a large number of photos. A bunch of slides with uncompressed photos is soon going to become unnecessarily bloated, take longer to load and may possibly cause problems when running as well. If you need to share the presentation it will take longer to send across cyberspace, so keeping image file sizes small is a good idea.

The only issue with JPEG is that the more compression is applied, the lower the quality of the image. However, even a small amount of compression

Fig 14. The image in the right-hand circle is compressed to 20% and is of noticeably lower quality with outlines becoming blurred and the telltale artefacts in the sky area that are a sure sign of a low-quality JPEG file.

is enough to lower the file size dramatically without noticeably affecting the image quality.

The three circular cutouts shown in Fig. 14 each show a detail of the larger image and you can see that there's not much difference in quality between the uncompressed image in the circle on the left and the one at 80% compression in the middle. The right-hand image is compressed to 20% and is of noticeably lower quality with outlines becoming blurred and the telltale artefacts in the sky area that are a sure sign of a low-quality JPEG file. But the difference in file size between the uncompressed image and the one at 80% is significant. The uncompressed image is over 6MB whereas the 80% compressed JPEG is 1.9MB, over three times smaller than the uncompressed image. A compression of about 80% quality is what I would recommend as an optimum for images being brought into your slide presentation.

JPEG is the most common image format you are likely to come across and I'll cover how you can optimise your images in the next section.

GIF

GIF is an older image format that only allows a palette of 256 colours. This makes it unsuitable for photos as it will not be able to address enough colours. This is especially true of images that have a lot of subtle shades where the colours will become very blocky.

It can be used when there are large areas of flat colour such as a logo and it also supports transparency allowing one colour in the image to be selected as the transparent channel although PNG would be more suitable for this.

GIF also supports crude animation. Whilst this might be more traditionally associated with unsophisticated clip art (who remembers the hamster dance?) it can also be employed to good effect when illustrating a process. The electricity generation slide is an example of this.

Example of using an animated GIF on a slide
Online at slidebook.tv/media/015

Fig 15: The image on the right shows the result when the image on the left is saved as a GIF file. The subtle shading of the sky has become blocky because the GIF file cannot address enough colours.

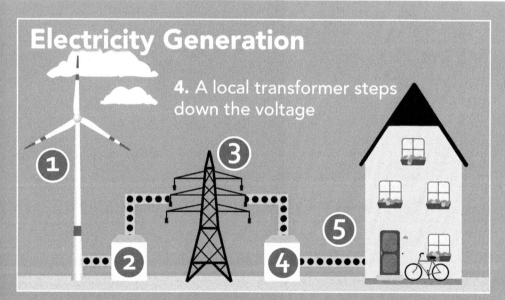

Slide 37. This slide illustrates electricity generation using an animated GIF image to show the direction of flow.

PNG

PNG is an image format that was introduced in 1996 as a replacement for GIF. The advantage it has over GIF is that, like JPEG, it supports 24-bit colour and so will give good quality on photos. The advantage it has over JPEG is that it supports transparency so that images can be cut out and placed on your slides.

Because PNG is a lossless format, it will create bigger files. So for straightforward photos, JPEG is the best choice. Unlike GIF, PNG does not support animation.

Slide 38   *Slide* 39

Slides 38 and 39. The first slide is a full-frame image. The second shows how an image can be cut out and placed on a background.

What about TIFF and RAW?

You may also come across TIFF and raw files. TIFF is a high-quality image format more likely to be associated with printing and it generates large files. If you've got a TIFF file that you want to use, save it as a JPEG before inserting it in to your presentation. You won't notice the difference in quality but it will make your presentation file size much smaller.

A raw file, as the name suggests, is the file format that your digital camera uses when capturing images from its internal sensor. There are many different raw formats as they tend to be device-dependent. Because they will contain all of the information captured by the camera, raw files tend to be very large. They are designed to be post-processed at which point a raw file will often be converted into JPEG.

Fig 16: One of these is TIFF and one is JPEG. Do you know which is which? The TIFF file size is ten times that of the JPEG.

Summary of image formats

Here's a useful summary table showing which image format to use for different purposes.

Square or rectangular photo	JPEG (compressed to 80% quality)
Cutout photograph	PNG with transparency applied
Flat colour logo	PNG or GIF
Simple animation	GIF

Image resolution

Another area that can be confusing to people is image resolution. Simply put, the resolution of an image is its width and height measured in pixels. You'll often hear digital cameras referred to by their resolution in megapixels (millions of pixels or MP for short). For example, a 12 MP resolution image might have height and width dimensions of 4,256 x 2,832 pixels. (Multiply these two together and you get 12,052,992 pixels.)

The main point about resolution as far as your slides are concerned is that it's another factor that will determine how bloated your presentation might become if you use images that are too high in resolution.

You can reduce file size and image resolution in both PowerPoint and Keynote but to my mind, it means that you are handing over control of your images to these programs and you might not like what they come up with. By default, PowerPoint will reduce the size of images brought into your presentation. That's probably not a bad thing if you're in the habit of importing very large digital camera images but if you're trying to optimise an image for a presentation then you don't want PowerPoint to muck about with it. The video link shows how you can quickly turn off image compression in PowerPoint so that you are in full control of the quality of your images.

Keynote will allow you to reduce the overall file size via the menu if you find that your presentation size is too large. But again I'd say it's best to get the images to the right size in the first place so that you don't have to take this step.

How to turn off image compression in PowerPoint Online at slidebook.tv/media/016

So what is the optimum image resolution that gives the best image quality with the lowest file size? Well, here's a rule of thumb that you can work to but of course you can experiment. My advice would be to aim for an image width of 1,600 pixels for an image that is to be used full screen.

If you're going to use the image smaller on the slide then you can make its pixel dimensions proportionally smaller.

An added bonus of using 1,600 pixels is that, if you are using a 16:9 ratio slide setup then it's easy to work out the dimensions for a full-frame image: 1,600 pixels x 900 pixels!

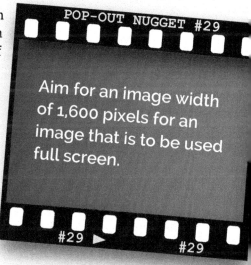

POP-OUT NUGGET #29

Aim for an image width of 1,600 pixels for an image that is to be used full screen.

#29 ▶   #29   #29

1,600 pixels wide   533 pixels wide

Fig 17. Use an image width of 1,600 pixels for a full screen image and proportionately smaller for smaller images.

Optimising images

So here's the practical bit. How do you optimise your images in practice? If you are used to working with any kind of image editing software then you may already be familiar with these techniques.

Optimising for file size and quality

I am going to assume we want to bring an image into our slide presentation and to use it full screen. In other words, we want an image 1,600 pixels wide at 80% JPEG quality.

To do this you can use any decent image editing software such as Photoshop. There are also a number of online tools that you can use for free. One such is Pixlr (**pixlr.com/editor**) and the video below runs through the process of optimising an image using Pixlr.

Optimising an image in Pixlr
Online at slidebook.tv/media/017

Cutout images

I've already talked about how you can use the PNG image format to place images on a transparent background which can be really effective. This can also be done in Pixlr and the video below runs through this process.

Because PNG files are much larger than JPEG, you need to be careful not to use a large number as it could make your file very big.

Producing a cutout image in Pixlr
Online at slidebook.tv/media/018

Keeping it legal

If you are producing a slide presentation to be used in any kind of professional environment it's essential to ensure that the images you are using are legal. (They should also be legal in a non-professional environment of course, but I'm not going to judge you if you lift a couple of images from the web to add to a slide presentation you're showing to your granny about your rambling holiday in Provence.)

POP-OUT NUGGET #30

Always make sure that you are using images legally and remember, Google Images is not a free stock library.

#30 ▶ #30

A client asked me to put together a slide presentation and they sent over several images to be added to some of the slides. I took a look at these images and they were quite a disparate bunch. My suspicions were immediately aroused. These didn't look like the sort of images a client would normally send. They were all different sizes, all very different subjects and of varying quality.

I was emailing the client about the presentation so I thought I would mention the images and ask where they had got them from. The reply was, "We got them from Google Images." To be honest, that reply didn't come as a big surprise. As I said, I had had my suspicions which is why I asked the question in the first place.

So I had to gently break the news that we couldn't actually use these images in the presentation. The client of course asked why. The simple answer is: Google Images is not a free stock library.

All of the images that appear on Google Images when you do a search have been produced by someone, either photographed or drawn or digitised in some way or another. The copyright in these images belongs to someone. Taking images and using them in your presentations is stealing. It might not seem as bad as popping down to your local Sainsbury's and half-inching a packet of digestive biscuits. But it's the same thing really, except that it is so much easier to pinch something from the screen in front of you.

Where to get images

Creative Commons

Some of the images that appear in the Google Images search results *can* be used. In the *Tools* menu you can select just those images that are labelled for re-use.

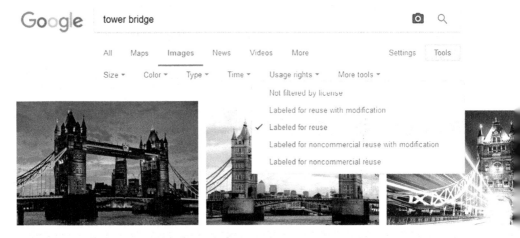

Fig 18. Selecting pictures in Google Images that are labelled for re-use.

Many of the results you'll get in Google Images if you select *Labeled for reuse* will be images that are on Creative Commons. Creative Commons is an organisation devoted to expanding the range of creative works available for others to build upon legally and to share. A Creative Commons (CC) license is a copyright license that enables the free distribution of an otherwise copyrighted work. A CC license is used when an author wants to give people the right to share, use, and build upon a work that they have created.

There may be terms and conditions attached to the re-use of an image so you will need to check this out. For example, an image might require attribution. This means that you will have to add a line of text to the slide attributing the image to the copyright holder. As one of our aims is to keep our slides free of unnecessary clutter, this is something best avoided if possible.

Public domain

Works in the public domain are those whose exclusive intellectual property rights have expired, have been forfeited or are inapplicable. For example, the works of Rembrandt or Chaucer are now in the public domain.

There are many sources of public domain images and a comprehensive list can be found at **commons.wikimedia.org/wiki/Commons:Free_media_resources/Photography**.

One example is Pixabay (**www.pixabay.com**) which has thousands of free-to-use images. Some of the pictures in this book have come from Pixabay.

Fig 19. The Haywain by John Constable was painted in 1821. It's free to use because the image is now in the public domain.

Stock images

There are also many stock image libraries that have vast numbers of high-quality images for a small cost. Shutterstock is one such example; it holds over 100 million stock images. Other big online stock image providers include Adobe Stock, iStockPhoto and Thinkstock.

The costs of using stock images are usually quite low. Each stock image provider will have its own variable pricing models but typically expect to pay about £5.00 per image.

They will also have different licences for the use of images, so do check that the license will allow you to use a specific image in your presentation. News-type pictures may only be sanctioned for editorial use so again check this before downloading a stock image.

Getting permission

If you find a picture that you really want to use that is not royalty-free, then the other option is to get permission from the copyright owner to use the picture. It may be a hassle to get hold of the copyright owner so it depends on how much you really want to use the image. If you do go down this route, make sure that you get their permission in writing; an email should suffice.

Fair use

There's also the concept of fair use or fair dealing as it is more likely to be called in the UK. Fair dealing exceptions specify purposes for which a reproduction of a work is permitted, without requiring the copyright owner's permission. I include it here only for completeness as there are plenty of other better avenues to go down when sourcing images than in getting involved in the potential quagmire of fair dealing.

Take photos yourself!

Finally of course, why not take the photos yourself? That way there are no copyright issues at all. The average smartphone can take superb pictures and the advantage of taking a picture yourself is that you can produce it exactly how you want it. The disadvantage of course is that if you're looking for a picture of someone standing on the top of Mount Everest then a stock photo is probably going to be your best bet, unless you fancy a quick trip over to Nepal!

POP-OUT NUGGET #31

There are many different ways to get good images legally (as well as for free, if not very cheap).

#31

#31

What to avoid and what to use

So we've dealt with the technical aspect of images and also how to source images. Now we come to the actual content itself – what sort of images to use. Not all images are created equal and there are some things that you should definitely steer clear of.

Let's get the things to avoid out of the way first.

Clip art

What I mean by clip art is the cheap and cheerful drawings that have been around since the dawn of computer graphics and which, to be honest, have no right calling themselves art. Whilst I am all for keeping things simple, I don't include in that the use of drawings that look as though they've been scribbled as part of a primary school art project.

The other type of image that also falls into this category is the ubiquitous 3D stick man. This colourless blob seems to get all over the place sucking the life out of many a presentation.

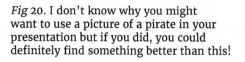

Fig 20. I don't know why you might want to use a picture of a pirate in your presentation but if you did, you could definitely find something better than this!

Fig 21. The ubiquitous stick man – one to be avoided.

Corporate-style images

Not quite in the same league as using Comic Sans font but not far off is the men-in-suits-with-perfect-teeth-boardroom-table-smiley-corporate image. You know the sort of thing I mean.

To me these are the visual equivalent of bullet points. The general thinking behind using this sort of image is: "We're in business and we're presenting a business presentation to business people so it obviously makes sense to use images of people in business!"

It's a lazy thing to do, but far more importantly, it won't inspire or wow your audience. Firstly because the use of that image is probably not going to be pertinent to the point you are trying to make, and secondly because your audience will have seen such images hundreds of times before.

There will be better ways of making your point.

Fig 22. The corporate, boardroom image – the visual equivalent of bullet points!

Clichés

This is what I mean by clichés:

Slide 40

Slide 41

Slide 42

Slide 43

Slide 44

Slides 40-44. A set of clichéd slides.

You can probably think of other image clichés that you see all the time and you won't need to sit through too many slide presentations until you've seen all of the above (probably more than once!) Need I say any more?

Other image no-nos

Low resolution, out-of-focus, poor quality images are clearly not acceptable but you know that already. When you see such an image in a presentation it almost certainly means it's been lifted from Google Images or from someone's website and so is not only ropey in quality but also probably being used illegally. I've even seen images being used in presentations that are the low-resolution stock library comps and that still have the library's watermark across them! What does that say about the presenter?

POP-OUT NUGGET #32

Avoid the use of tacky clip art, stick men, corporate-style business images and clichéd images.

#32 ▶   #32

- ▶ They are a cheapskate. It would have only cost a few quid to buy the image.

- ▶ They don't care about the quality of the images they are presenting to their audience.

- ▶ They haven't read this book!

One final thing. If you are using images to represent technology, make sure they are images of current tech and not a phone, tablet, computer, etc., from even a couple of years ago. If you're using a slide presentation that you created some time back then it's worth checking that the images you have used are still current and relevant.

POP-OUT NUGGET #33

Low resolution, out-of-focus, poor quality images are clearly not acceptable.

#33 ▶   #33

So what kind of images should be used to get the most impact?

The specific images you use in your presentation totally depend on what you are trying to convey. It's much easier for me to advise on *what not to use* than on what you should be using because what not to use applies to every slide presentation.

POP-OUT NUGGET #34

When using an image make sure it's impactful, colourful, quirky, different and amusing. And that it RICEs your slides!

#34 ▶   #34

So firstly a few guidelines on the attributes of a good image:

- ▶ It is impactful.

- ▶ It is colourful (although purely monochrome images across a presentation can also work well).

- ▶ It is quirky.

- ▶ It is different (or even unique).

- ▶ It is amusing.

- ▶ And most important of all, it reinforces, illustrates, clarifies or explains the point you are trying to make.

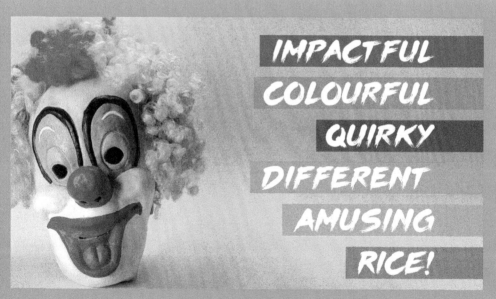

IMPACTFUL
COLOURFUL
QUIRKY
DIFFERENT
AMUSING
RICE!

Slide 45. This slide ticks all the boxes (unless of course you suffer from coulrophobia, in which case it's probably not particularly amusing).

Not all images will have all of these attributes (apart from the obligatory final one) but if you can tick some of these boxes then it suggests that your image is on the right track.

A couple of other ideas

Why not try adding an image to your presentation that you shot today? I got this idea from Eamonn O'Brien (**www.thereluctantspeakersclub.com**) who successfully uses this technique in some of his presentations. It shouldn't be shoehorned in but used as part of the flow of the presentation. You'll also need to have access to your presentation to insert this last minute picture so if you've had to hand your slides over to an AV company in advance then it might not be possible to do it. However, if you can do this, it adds a talking point to the presentation and is something people are likely to remember afterwards.

To take it one step further, some speakers like to take candid pictures of the audience at the event and add these to their presentation. If this technique can be added to your talk to provide entertainment or help to tell your story, then again, it's a way of engaging the audience and giving them something to talk about and remember.

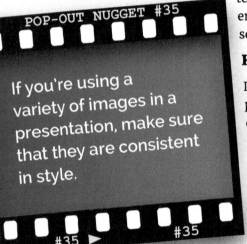

POP-OUT NUGGET #35

If you're using a variety of images in a presentation, make sure that they are consistent in style.

Keep them consistent

If you're using a variety of images in a presentation, make sure that there is a consistency within the selection of images or the way in which they are being used. I'm not saying that they all have to be the same subject, location, people, etc., but try not to end up with a clashing hotchpotch of images that make your presentation look fragmented and disjointed.

Image usage techniques

It's all well and good using the right image on a slide but if it's not used on the slide in the right way it can make your presentation look bland and samey. Here are a few useful techniques to help you optimise the use of images on your slides.

Fill the slide

How many times have you seen something like this?

Slide 46. A typical title slide with picture.

A lot I'll wager, and the reason is that it's the way that PowerPoint encourages you to do it. Why waste all the space around the image. Fill the slide with the image and place the text on top.

You'll need to ensure that the image has the space to overlay the text and you might need to add a black or white glow around the text or put it inside a box to lift in from the background image as illustrated in the healthy eating slides in chapter four. Slide 47 looks far more professional and has far more impact than slide 46 and you'll also notice that doing it this way allows us to use a bigger font size for the title.

POP-OUT NUGGET #36

Don't waste space on a slide. Try filling the slide with your image and placing the text on top.

#36 ▶

#36

Slide 47. How much better does it look when the picture fills the frame and the title is overlaid on top.

Bleed off

It's not always possible or indeed desirable to fill the slide with an image but a technique that can work well and help to lift an image is to bleed it off the edge of the slide.

The top slide is pretty good but the image has been placed on the left in its black box with the text on the right. On the second slide, the image has been cut out and then bled off the left hand edge of the slide adding to the menace of the man's face.

Bleeding off the image also has the added benefit of giving us more space on the rest of the slide as well as showing that the image has been used creatively and thoughtfully rather than just plonked on the slide.

Don't squash and squeeze

Another thing people sometimes do is to squash or squeeze an image to make it fit the space allowed for it and it's usually very obvious when this has been done. When resizing an image, make sure you do it proportionately by grabbing and dragging the corner handles and not the handles in the middle.

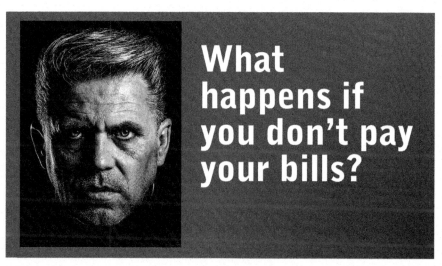

Slide 48. This slide is quite good and looks menacing.

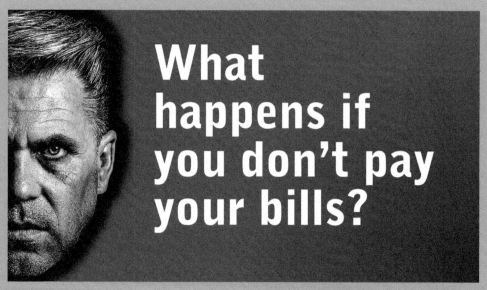

Slide 49. But bleeding off the face on the left of the slide adds to the threat and impact.

If the shape of the image doesn't fit into the space you've allowed for it then crop the image. This is very easy to do in PowerPoint as you saw in the video link in chapter four and there are some added features within the crop tool in PowerPoint to make it even more versatile.

Cut it out!

Using a cutout image can make a slide look more polished and professional and again, frees up more room on the slide.

The first title slide below doesn't look too bad but cutting out the ballerina makes it look so much more elegant and clean. It also allows us to enlarge the figure and place her toes right at the bottom of the slide, using the base of the slide as the stage.

There are various ways of implementing a cutout of an image in your slides. Many stock images already come with a transparent background so these can be imported straight into your slides – job done! Other stock images are shot with the object isolated on a white background which makes them easier to cut out. When searching for an image in a stock library, try adding the word *isolated* to your search query.

You can cut out the image in photo editing software and save as a PNG with a transparent background before importing it into your slide software. This is easier to do if your image has a clearly defined background.

You can also cut out parts of an image within PowerPoint and Keynote. It works well in PowerPoint where there are contiguous areas of flat colour as the screencast demonstrates.

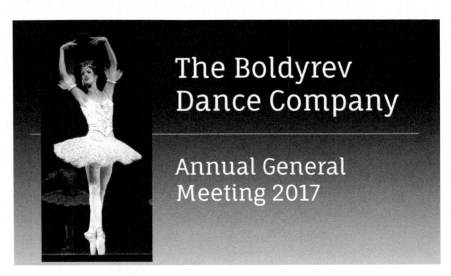

Slide 50. A typical title slide with the image placed on top.

The Boldyrev Dance Company

Annual General Meeting 2017

Slide 51. How much more elegant and professional does it look with the dancer cut out on the background?

How to cut out an image in PowerPoint
Online at slidebook.tv/media/019

Panning

When you've got a very long or very wide image and you need to show it all, another useful technique is to pan the image. For example, you may want show a web page in your presentation or maybe a panoramic scene. I'm going to go into more detail about the use of animations in your slides in chapter ten but the screencast below shows how to pan images in PowerPoint.

How to pan images in PowerPoint
Online at slidebook.tv/media/020

Put on a mask

Another useful technique is to use masking to highlight the part of the image that you want to talk about. This is slightly more complex but it can be really effective if used in the right way. Again it can be especially useful to highlight elements on a screen grab but it can be used anywhere you need to pick out a part of an image.

In the image on the right we've focused in on a detail of a painting and then masked that detail. (The painting is the hell panel from *The Garden of Earthly Delights* by Hieronymus Bosch. The masked section shows what is alleged to be a self-portrait of Bosch under a table.)

The masking method involves duplicating an image, cropping the top image and then fading back the bottom image. The screencast link on the right shows exactly how it's done in PowerPoint.

Slide 52. Masking is a useful technique for highlighting a part of an image.

How to mask an image in PowerPoint
Online at slidebook.tv/media/021

The Rule of Thirds

A phrase first coined by the English painter and engraver John Thomas Smith in the 18th Century, the *Rule of Thirds* is a compositional rule of thumb that imagines an image as being divided into thirds, both horizontally and vertically. Prominent compositional elements are then positioned along these lines. It is claimed that that aligning a subject with these points creates more interest in the composition.

A bonus to this technique is that when designing slides it can be especially useful as it gives us the space to add other elements such as text to the slide as Slide 53 shows.

Fig 23: In the first picture with both the fisherman and the bank centred, the image looks flat and uninteresting. Moving both to intersect with lines dividing the image into thirds gives the picture more tension and impact

Slide 53. A title slide that uses an image adhering to the Rule of Thirds.

CHAPTER SEVEN

Presenting Data

An area where people often struggle when building a slide presentation is when they have to present data. What is the best method of conveying the meaning and significance of the data? How do you present data in a way that is not confusing and is clear to the audience?

It's usually a matter of referring to the trusty chart tools in PowerPoint or Keynote and there's nothing wrong with that. The chart tools in PowerPoint are much better and more intuitive than they used to be. If you have to present a lot of data quickly they are your best bet.

You may be unsurprised to learn that I will often steer clear of using the chart tools, preferring instead to keep things as simple as possible and totally under my control when adding chart data to a slide, more on this later.

Do you really need a chart?

At this point I'll refer you back to RICE as it's especially applicable to the use of chart or data slides. You've been given a bunch of figures to present but what is the significance of those figures to the audience? For example, let's say you've got the sales figures for Henson Wines for the last four quarters along with the amount contributed by each of three sales people to those figures. It would make sense to show them something like slide 54 wouldn't it?

POP-OUT NUGGET #37

Consider what information you want to convey, then decide how best to present that information so that it reinforces, illustrates, clarifies or explains your point.

#37 ▶   #37

But what point are you actually trying to make? If the point is to show that overall sales have grown by more than 20% in the last quarter then this chart is too complex and most of the information in it is superfluous. You could use a much simpler chart to show a 20% growth from one quarter to another, you could be more creative, which I talk about a bit further on in this chapter or maybe you don't need to use a chart at all (or even a slide).

Consider what information you want to convey and then decide how best to present that information so that it reinforces, illustrates, clarifies or explains your point.

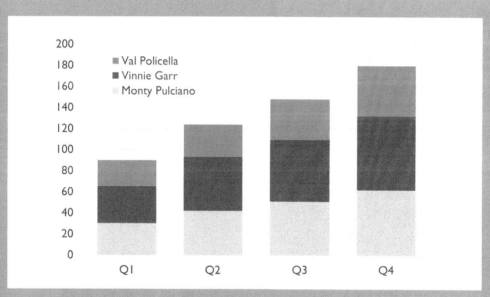

Slide 54. Henson Wines sales chart.

Types of chart

We'll assume that you've decided that you definitely need to use a chart to convey the data you have. What sort of chart should you use? This page is a bit like going back to school I'll admit, and I won't give you 100 lines or make you stand in the corner if you decide to skip over it, but think of it as a refresher!

Line graph

A line graph is good to show changes over a period of time. Trends can more easily be shown when using a line graph. To maintain the clarity of a line graph, always use solid lines and don't plot too many lines on one chart.

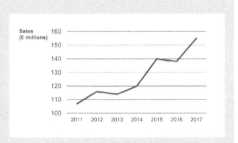

Fig 24. A line graph.

Bar graphs

A bar graph can be vertical or horizontal. When it's vertical it is often called a column chart. They are basically the same beast but it's useful to use a bar chart when you need to show negative figures or when you have long data labels as shown in the bottom example.

Bar graphs are used to show a comparison of different items or over different time periods.

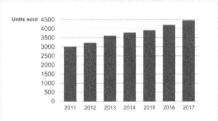

Fig 25. A vertical bar graph.

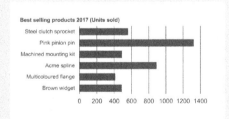

Fig 26. A horizontal bar graph.

Stacked bar graph

This should be used to compare many different items and show the composition of each item being compared.

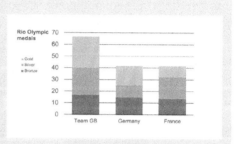

Fig 27. A stacked bar graph.

A stacked bar graph is a graph that is used to break down and compare parts of a whole, with each bar in the chart representing the whole. The composition of the whole is represented by the different sized segments within it.

Pie chart

A pie chart is used to show how different parts make up the whole. It is then easy to see how much each segment has contributed to the 100% of the whole. To make the comparison easier to see, the segments should be arranged in size order either largest to smallest or the other way around.

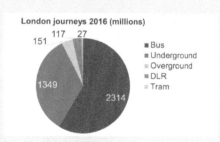

Fig 28. A pie chart.

Keeping it simple

The best way of keeping things simple is to use the chart tools built into PowerPoint or Keynote. There is a lot of flexibility and features within these tools and you should be able to create charts that are perfectly serviceable for your presentation.

It's not the purpose of this book to be a complete training manual for either PowerPoint or Keynote and there is plenty of online help that will take you through the process of adding charts in either program so I'm not going to go into any detail of how to design charts using the chart tools.

Suffice it to say that, as with all tools, they should be used with care and you should endeavour to optimise your charts by keeping them as simple as possible whilst making sure there is enough information to convey the significance of the data.

However, there are times when it is easier or better to add the chart manually to your presentation, drawing everything by hand. Why would anyone want to do that when it's so much quicker to use the chart tools? Well, there are a few reasons:

▶ You want to design a creative chart that is outside the capabilities of the chart tools.

▶ You want total control of the exact positioning and size of all of the chart elements.

▶ You want to be able to do build sequences in a way that the chart tools won't let you.

It's actually as quick to do this anyway, if you know a few simple techniques. On the right is an example of a chart that was designed manually.

Whilst it clearly has creative elements to it, it also contains some of the standard elements of a normal bar chart:

▶ Gridlines

▶ Y axis labels

▶ X axis labels

▶ X axis title (contained in the slide title)

▶ Data labels

Slide 55. This beer consumption graph has been produced in a creative way to get the point across.

Whilst it is possible in PowerPoint to create all of this using the chart tools and then remove the bars, to my mind it is much better to do this sort of thing manually so that you have full control over all of the elements on the slide. The screencast below takes you through the full process of creating the chart shown above.

How to manually produce the beer chart in PowerPoint
Online at slidebook.tv/media/022

Sometimes complexity is necessary

I'm all for keeping things as simple as possible but I'm not saying that a slide can never be complex. I've produced slides in the past for the pharma industry where they are presenting drug trial data. Some of this is necessarily complex but there is a key point here: Both the presenter and the audience were in the pharma industry and understood the data that was being presented as well as the complexity in the data.

If you need to use a complex diagram or chart then there are three things to be aware of:

▶ Ensure that the chart is comprehensible to all audience members. Don't make it more complex than it has to be.

▶ Ensure that it is readable. There is a temptation to make everything small on the slide when you have a lot of information. Remember my point from earlier – everyone in the room should be able to read the text on your slides.

▶ If you can, use a build sequence to construct the slide. Bring in each relevant part of the chart or diagram one piece at a time and speak about each element before moving on to the next.

I am often asked to clean up slides that a client has created and invariably this will include complex charts or diagrams. Once I have established what the client is trying to convey with the slide (and that's the important point) I can usually make a marked improvement.

Hans Rosling

If you want a great example of someone who uses complexity in a stunningly impressive way then take a look at the presentations given by Hans Rosling. There's a link to an example video below of a TED Talk

Hans Rosling - The best stats you've ever seen
Online at slidebook.tv/media/023

given by him in 2006. His organisation Gapminder has developed software that takes masses of socio-economic data and turns it into animated, meaningful presentations. The visuals are complex but he explains them in a compelling way and he uses the animation built into the software to make the data sing. It is data that would otherwise be hidden as a mass of meaningless figures, so to turn this data into something that opens minds and debunks myth is a ground-breaking thing to do.

Be creative

Whilst the chart tools in PowerPoint and Keynote are adequate for producing good-quality charts and graphs, creatively presenting facts and figures will be more memorable than a bunch of bars, lines and pies.

Can your data be presented in a more creative way? On the next five pages are examples of creative data presentation that I hope might inspire you to think about how you can best present the data that you have. Bear in mind that the win-win is that, not only will this creativity make your slides more memorable and effective, it will also make them more fun to work on in the first place!

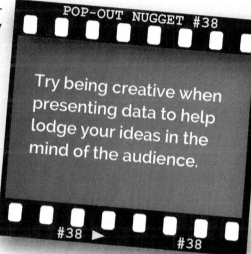

POP-OUT NUGGET #38

Try being creative when presenting data to help lodge your ideas in the mind of the audience.

#38 ▶ #38

"The prize money for the Wimbledon's men's singles has risen over 14 fold in the last 30 years. In 1985 the prize stood at £130,000. Over the next ten years it almost tripled to a value of £365,000. The next decade saw a less dramatic rise but by 2005 the prize money was at £630,000. And in the last ten years up to 2015 it has seen another threefold rise, standing at nearly £1.9 million."

In this sequence of slides, the balls get larger as the prize money goes up. The slide shows the third in the sequence. There's a link to the full animated sequence of this slide and the others on these five pages in chapter ten in the section dealing with animations.

Slide 56. Wimbledon prize money chart.

"There are over 3 million hectares of woodland in the UK. Northern Ireland has the lowest area of planted woodland at just 112,000 hectares. Wales is about 50% larger than Northern Ireland but has nearly three times the area of planted woodland. The largest country in the UK, England, doesn't have the largest area of woodland. At about 1.3 million hectares it's behind Scotland which, despite being less than two-thirds the size of England, has 10% more woodland."

For this slide I took the picture of the tree rings, made it 1,600 x 900 pixels and added it into the background of the slide. Then I took the same image and cut out a section around the edge of one of the tree rings and added that to the slide. In between the two images I sandwiched a pie chart slightly bigger than the cut hole and made the slices semi-transparent so that the tree rings underneath showed through.

Slide 57. Woodland area chart.

 "It may be a worst-case scenario for sea level rise, but it is possible that levels could rise by nearly a metre over the course of the twenty-first century."

Take a look at the animation of this slide when you get to chapter ten. It's a fairly simple line chart, but the movement helps bring it to life and get the message across.

Slide 58. Sea rise chart.

"The numbers of lions in the world has declined dramatically over the last 200 years. In 1800 there were 1.2 million lions in the wild. Numbers fell steadily over the 19th century and into the first half of the 20th century and by the 1940s, stood at 450,000. But the decline accelerated after that and by the 1980s the number of lions had fallen to just 100,000. 10 years later the number had halved to 50,000. And by the beginning of the 21st century, there were just 20,000 lions left in the wild, one-sixtieth the number of 200 years ago."

This sequence of slides is really simple, but the gradually disappearing lion graphics really help emphasise the decline in lion numbers over the last two centuries.

Slide 59. Declining lion population chart.

"The UK now produces some great wines but we've got a long way to go before we are anywhere near other wine-producing countries in terms of the amounts produced. Taking two examples, you can see that both France and the USA are each producing a lot more wine than us."

Finally a variation of a pie chart. The coloured areas for each country still show the proportions but in a more creative way.

Slide 60. Wine production chart.

PRODUCTION
DIRECTOR...
CAMERA ...
DATE

CHAPTER EIGHT

Video

If images are engaging then it probably stands to reason that video is even more engaging. It's certainly true online. Take Facebook for example. A simple text status update will get less engagement than an image in a Facebook post and likewise an image will get less engagement than video. You've probably heard many people extolling the virtues of using video online and rightly so, because it works.

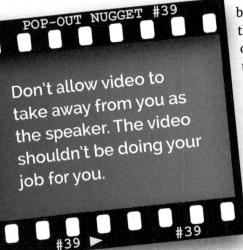

POP-OUT NUGGET #39

Don't allow video to take away from you as the speaker. The video shouldn't be doing your job for you.

#39 ▶ #39

Using video in your slide deck can also work, but you have to use it much more carefully than you would online. As with any aspect of your presentation, a video must work in the context of the talk you are giving and must definitely meet the RICE aims.

One thing a video shouldn't do is take away from you as a speaker. Don't have the video do your job for you. If you're showing a video of someone saying something that you could easily say then drop it and say it yourself. An exception might be if you are showing a video of someone famous putting across a viewpoint. The point may well be reinforced in the audience's mind if it is being put across by a recognised authority.

Generally, video should be shown in small snippets. If you are giving a fifteen-minute speech, you don't want to have seven or eight minutes of it taken up with video.

Technical aspects

Unless you are playing a silent movie then you are going to need speakers. Check if the venue has a sound system and, if not, take your own speakers along. Make sure that they are loud enough to be heard at the back of the room.

The copyright rules that I have already covered for images also apply to videos. Make sure that you are not using any footage illegally.

Don't use an external video player on your computer to play the video. Switching out of PowerPoint or Keynote to another program interrupts the flow of your presentation and should be avoided wherever possible. (On this point I would also advise that you shouldn't toggle in and out of PowerPoint or Keynote to another program unless you really have to. Try to keep your presentation self-contained within whichever software you are using. If your presentation involves demonstrating a piece of software or a website then it may be something you would have to do but it should be avoided if possible.)

POP-OUT NUGGET #40

Don't use an external video player to play video. Switching out of PowerPoint or Keynote to another program interrupts the flow of your presentation.

#40 ▶   #40

Bringing video into PowerPoint

There are two ways of getting video into PowerPoint but only one that I would recommend. You can either embed the file in the presentation or you can link to an online file and it's the embedding method that I would recommend.

Linking to an online file gives you access to millions of videos across the internet but you need to be completely sure that you are going to have a robust internet connection if you are going to use this method. If you are presenting at your own premises and you are confident of your internet connection then there is no reason why you shouldn't use this method. If you are presenting somewhere else then it's always better to have the video embedded in case there is an issue with the connection. Alternatively you could have a backup in case the video doesn't work.

There are two ways of playing a video in PowerPoint. You can either directly embed it which means that the video becomes part of the presentation or you can link to a video file stored on your PC which means it remains external to the presentation. There are pros and cons to each method.

If you directly embed it in your presentation then it will add significantly to the file size of the presentation but it means that you won't have to remember to include the separate video file with your presentation which is especially useful if you are having to send the presentation file to someone else.

If you link the file then your presentation file size will remain small. However, it also means that you will have to ensure that the video file is on the computer and in the same folder from which it was originally linked. This can cause issues should you have to send the files elsewhere.

Both methods are shown in the screencast below.

How to embed and link a video file in PowerPoint
Online at slidebook.tv/media/024

CHAPTER NINE

A Case Study

What's wrong with this?

Let's finish this section with a case study that takes all of the learnings from this part of the book and demonstrates them in a real-life presentation. Its starting point is a presentation which you can see is in need of some drastic improvement.

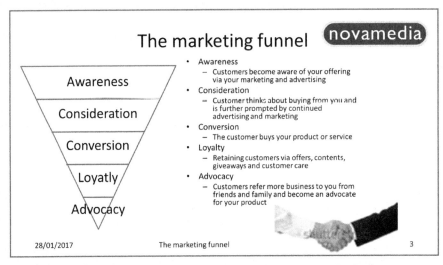

Slide 61. The marketing funnel presentation. What's wrong with this?

You're no doubt thinking that looks terrible and of course you'd be right. Now watch the video below to see how this is used by the presenter when giving his talk.

The bad marketing funnel presentation
Online at slidebook.tv/media/025

That was exciting wasn't it?

Let's try a little exercise. There are many things wrong with that presentation; in fact there are seventeen things wrong with it. Before turning over the page where I have listed these things, use the table below to list the things you think are wrong with this presentation.

1	
2	
3	
4	
5	
6	
7	
8	
9	
10	
11	
12	
13	
14	
15	
16	
17	

These are the seventeen things I think are wrong with the marketing funnel presentation:

1	Too much text on the slide
2	The text is too small
3	The speaker dictated the text
4	The speaker did not use builds to bring in each part of the funnel one at a time
5	Spelling error – *Loyalty* is spelt wrong
6	The handshake is a poor quality image
7	It's also an awful, clichéd stock image
8	And it's being used illegally
9	The date is shown on the slide
10	The presentation title is shown on the slide at the bottom
11	The speaker has inserted a slide number
12	The company logo is shown on the slide
13	The design is very boring!
14	The fonts are standard, boring fonts
15	The animation on the title is unnecessary and tacky
16	The funnel graphic is far too simplistic
17	The speaker has confused the slide with his handout

How many of those did you get?

If you really want to get interactive, why not have a go now at designing a slide presentation that improves on Slide 61. If you just want to see how I think it could be done, turn over and read on.

Slide 62. A good start – getting the background right.

Making it better!

So how can we improve the presentation? The first thing we'll look at is the design. Rather than using a bright white background, I've chosen a clean, simple, graduated blue background.

The marketing funnel

Slide 63. Adding a title, but is this the right font?

Then we can add the title at the top. We could simply place the title in the centre using the default font but in white so it stands out like this.

Slide 64. A better title. A cleaner font and moved to the top right of the slide, giving us more room for the content.

The font used on the previous slide is Calibri and it's clean and readable but it's the default Microsoft Office font and has become so ubiquitous now that it's quite a boring font to use. Let's change it to another nice, clean font and move it to the top right of the slide. This font is called Eurostile and placing the title at the top right gives us more space for our funnel graphic.

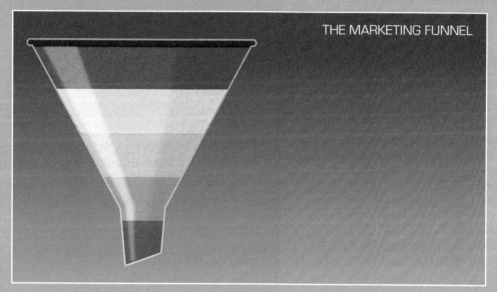

Slide 65. Adding in the funnel graphic.

So far, so good. We also decided that the funnel graphic was boring and poorly designed so I created a simple funnel graphic that suited my purposes for this presentation, clearly banded in five separate colours for the five parts of the funnel process.

What about making the presentation more personable by introducing a human element to the slides? It has to be the same person throughout so I needed to find a stock image or set of stock images of one person that I could use to help illustrate the five stages of the funnel. It wasn't easy to find stock images that fitted the bill, but I did manage to find one in the end. However, it would have been a fairly simple job to find a willing volunteer and shoot the photos myself for the fives poses.

With the addition of a couple of other stock images, I was then able to quickly finish the presentation and the final slides can be seen on the right.

Watch the full animated version in the video below.

The good marketing funnel presentation
Online at slidebook.tv/media/026

These are the slides that make up the presentation:

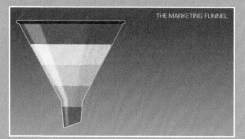

Slide 66

Slide 67

Slide 68

Slide 69

Slide 70

Slide 71

Slide 72

Slide 73

Slides 66–73. The full marketing funnel presentation.

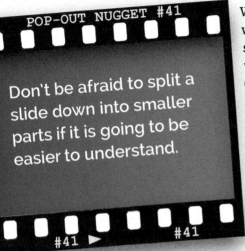

POP-OUT NUGGET #41

Don't be afraid to split a slide down into smaller parts if it is going to be easier to understand.

#41 ▶   #41

What makes this better? Well, the first thing we can say is that we have addressed all seventeen points in the list of things that were wrong with the original presentation. Go through that list again and you'll see what I mean.

The first presentation was just one slide, whereas our improved slide deck consisted of eight separate slides. Don't be afraid to split a slide down into smaller parts if it is going to be easier to understand. One of the problems with the first presentation is that the audience were likely reading ahead of the speaker and they would probably get to the end of the text well before the speaker had finished delivering it.

Slides vs. handouts revisited

Point seventeen in our list of the things that were wrong with the presentation was that the speaker had confused their slides with their handouts. As you'll remember from chapter five, the golden rule is to keep your slides and handouts completely separate so that the slides work for your presentation and the handouts work as something to take away after your talk.

Because we have kept the text on our revised slides to a minimum, they won't work as handouts if printed out and given to the audience. Therefore we need to create a separate handout that the audience can take away with them afterwards. The handout I have designed for our marketing funnel presentation is shown below.

It still contains the funnel graphic to tie up with the slides as well as a repeat of the images of the man on the right. More importantly it contains the text to explain each part of the funnel process. Where our slides averaged under eight words each, the handout contains 75 words, which is fine because people can take it away and read it in their own time.

Fig 29. The handout for the marketing funnel presentation.

Section
FOUR

Putting on a show

By this stage you should have a pretty good idea of how to produce a slide presentation that is really effective content-wise and will not bore your audience to tears. This final section of the book is all about putting on a show.

Chapter ten deals with the use of animations and transitions and how to use them effectively to lift your presentation to an even higher level.

The final chapter will cover the issues involved in presenting your talk with slides at the venue.

Bringing it All to Life

Transitions and animations

When it comes to the use of animations in slide presentations my response would be a bit like Captain Rum's in the Blackadder episode "Potato". Blackadder asks Rum about the whereabouts of the crew, saying "I was under the impression that it was common maritime practice for a ship to have a crew." Rum's reply is "Opinion is divided on the subject. All the other captains say it is; I say it isn't."

POP-OUT NUGGET #42

Used creatively, animations can add an extra dimension to your slides that will help to wow your audience and make your presentation more memorable.

#42 ▶   #42

Many books I have read on using PowerPoint say that you shouldn't use animations. I say you should.

Of course I qualify that by saying that animations should be used sparingly and creatively. Once again, if you are in any doubt about the use of an animation in a slide presentation then simply apply RICE. Does the use of the animation help to reinforce, illustrate, clarify or explain the point you are making?

Transitions

Before moving on to cover animations, I first want to talk about transitions. A transition is how one slide blends into the next and this is where I would definitely advise complete simplicity. My personal preference is to set all of the slides to fade which is a nice clean way of moving from one slide to another. There are a lot of whizzy transitions in PowerPoint and the only time I would suggest using anything other than a simple fade or cut is maybe on a title slide for effect.

POP-OUT NUGGET #43

Keep slide transitions simple.

#43 ▶   #43

Animations

We've already seen, in the title of the original marketing funnel slide, how a completely unnecessary animation lends absolutely nothing to a presentation. It can be really easy to get carried away with the use of animations. You may think you are being uber-creative, when in fact all you're doing is adding superfluous noise to your slide deck.

Used creatively however, animations can add an extra dimension to your slides that will help to wow your audience and, more importantly, help to make your presentation more memorable and therefore more effective.

Using builds

The most obvious use of animations is to create a build sequence as we have already seen in the improved marketing funnel presentation. Just showing your audience the information that you are currently addressing means that they will be focused on the point you are making and allows you to reinforce that point.

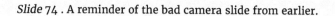

Camera Features

- It contains a large bright display that can easily be seen in full sunlight
- Multiple exposure modes that gives you full control of how you want to shoot
- The camera has an ergonomic design that feels more comfortable to hold
- 7 frames per second burst speed allows you to capture all the action
- 4K video at the flick of a switch allowing you to swap between still and movie modes

Slide 74 . A reminder of the bad camera slide from earlier.

More often than not a build sequence is associated with a set of bullet points showing one bullet at a time as the speaker addresses each point. Whilst this is marginally better than showing all of the text on the slide at once, it's still using bullets and text and it's still unengaging, boring and ineffective. You'll remember the camera bullet slide from earlier. Introducing a build sequence and showing one bullet at a time is just putting lipstick on a pig; it's still going to be a pig! Building the information one point at a time is still important, but do it in a more creative way as we did with the camera slides.

Large bright display

Slide 75. A reminder of one of the good camera slides from earlier and the use of creative builds.

If you were sitting in the audience, which version would grab your attention and be more memorable?

If you are showing a bar graph then you might want to address each bar individually building up to the final bar. Again, what you are doing is showing only what you need to show on screen to get your message across.

Creative animation

You can have great fun being creative with animations as long as your creativity doesn't distract from your message and, more importantly, that the addition of creative elements helps to RICE your message. If there's a bit of purposeful movement on the slide this can often help it to stick in people's minds. Lets's look at some examples where creativity has been used to help bring slides to life. I'll start with a repeat of the ecommerce payment process slide (Slide 3 from chapter one), as this is a great example of the use of animation to break down a slide and to make complex information clearer.

Slide 76. A reminder of the payment process slides from earlier in the book. A great example of the use of animation to break down a slide and to make complex information clearer.

The payment process slide revisted
Online at slidebook.tv/media/027

Then let's move on to our five creative data charts from earlier. These all use animations to help build the data as the speaker is addressing each point as well as to give the slides more impact.

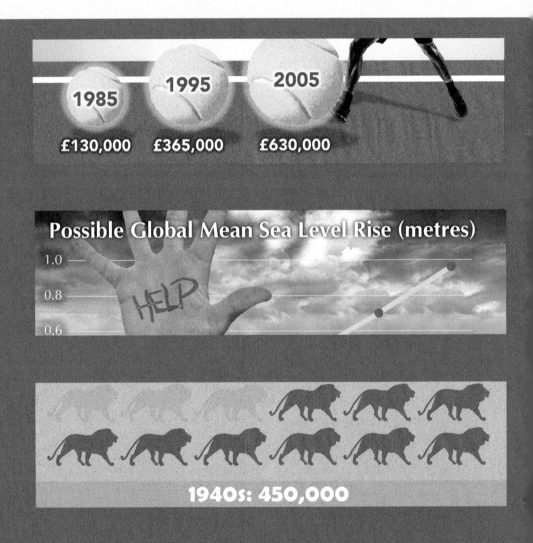

Fig 30. Our graphical charts from earlier all use creative animations. Check out the video opposite to see them in all their glory.

Total Woodland Area in the UK
(Thousands of hectares)

N. Ireland
112

WINE

PRODUCTION

How does the

UK
Just 425

USA
3,300

The five creative data charts in one video
Online at slidebook.tv/media/028

The slide below was one that I created for the eminent speaker Phillip Khan-Panni. If you watch the video you'll see how the glass fills as Phillip talks about the point he is conveying to the audience.

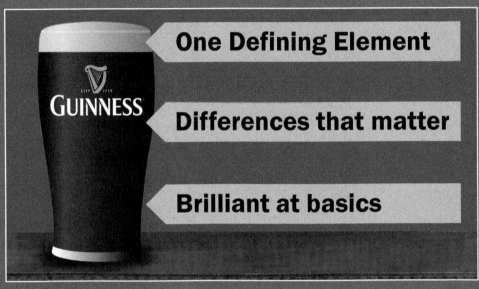

Slide 77. Animated pint of Guinness.

The pint of Guinness slide
Online at slidebook.tv/media/029

And finally just one more, a short, smooth animation with music in the background.

Slide 78. Another example of slide animation. .

The lipstick slide with music
Online at slidebook.tv/media/030

CHAPTER ELEVEN

Putting it All Together

Be prepared

I'm sure you've heard of the five Ps: *Perfect preparation prevents poor performance*. It's a hackneyed old phrase, but no less relevant for that. After all the hard work you've put in to construct the perfect slide deck that's going to have your audience cheering from the rafters, the last thing you want to do is mess it all up because you are underprepared.

Your preparation will depend upon the kind of venue and event you are speaking at. For a small-scale event you may have to take all of your own equipment and set it up. At the other end of the scale, a large conference at a prestigious location for example, all of the tech stuff will probably be handled by an AV company. Even if it's the latter you should still check that they will provide everything you need. You might also be presenting in a boardroom-style environment where you will have to link your laptop up to a large screen or TV. Let's explore these scenarios.

Small venue / event

If I'm speaking at a small event or venue then I'll take all of my equipment with me, even if the organisers say that they will have some or all of it at the venue. It'll sit in the boot of my car ready for deployment should it become necessary. Of course, in some cases you might be presenting at an event where you are the only speaker and you're expected to take and set up all your own gear.

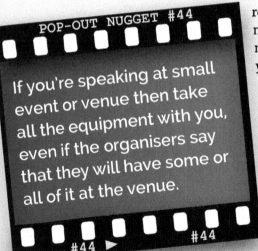

POP-OUT NUGGET #44

If you're speaking at small event or venue then take all the equipment with you, even if the organisers say that they will have some or all of it at the venue.

#44 ▶ #44

Typically, a small venue or event will have the projector propped on a table with the cable running across the floor and the projector screen at the front of the room smack in the middle of the stage. It may be that you can have no influence over this and it may be rude to suggest changes to your host, but an ideal setup for a small venue is to keep the projector down low and the screen up high with both offset to the side of the room.

Having it offset to the side means that the speaker can stand in the middle of the room to address the audience. Having the screen up high and the projector down low means that the screen is visible to everyone in the audience and the projector is not blocking anyone's view of the speaker or screen.

A typical setup

The ideal setup

Fig 31. A comparison of a typical room projector set-up and the ideal configuration.

If you can arrange for this sort of setup you may find that the projector can't be tilted up enough to display on the screen. My very low-tech solution is to carry a few small pieces of wood (or anything else that will fit the bill) that can be placed under the front of the projector to angle it up higher. All digital projectors will allow you to correct the keystoning that occurs when you tilt the projector upwards with the simple press of a button.

Fig 32. Keystone correction buttons on a projector remote. If the edges of your slide are skewed upwards or downwards on the screen, the keystone buttons on the projector or remote can be used to correct this.

Slide 79. A line-up slide to help get your slides straight on the screen.

A device I employ that is really helpful when it comes to setting up the slides on a screen is the use of a line-up slide. This can either be inserted as the first slide of your presentation or you can keep a separate line-up slide presentation on your laptop ready to use. The line-up slide that I have created is quite simple, as you can see.

It's a good tool to use to ensure:

▶   Your slides fill the screen.

▶   Your slides are square on the screen.

▶   There is no keystoning on your slides.

You can download the line-up slide for use in your presentations from the following URLs:

▶   16:9 ratio: slidebook.tv/media/031

▶   4:3 ratio: slidebook.tv/media/032

I always feel more comfortable if I can see the venue beforehand but this isn't always possible, especially if it is a distance away. Being relaxed and familiar with where you are going to present will ease some of the tension felt before stepping up in front of an audience. If you can't get to the venue beforehand then you should at least get there early so that you can familiarise yourself with the surroundings and set up and check the equipment.

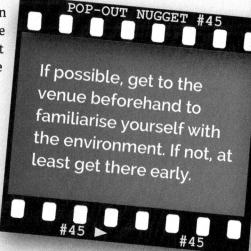

POP-OUT NUGGET #45

If possible, get to the venue beforehand to familiarise yourself with the environment. If not, at least get there early.

#45 ▶   #45

Being familiar with the equipment is another aspect of making life easier for yourself. Even at a small event there will usually be someone who is in charge of the equipment and who will ensure that you can easily get set up and have a quick run through with your slides.

When you're running through the slides you have an opportunity to test that everything is working as it should be. If not, you can then take any remedial action. If you are using audio, make sure the speakers are working and that the volume is optimised for people both at the front and back of the room.

Finally, make sure that the screen saver is disabled on the presentation laptop so that it doesn't come on in the middle of your presentation.

Checklist for small venue presentation

Here's a checklist of the things you'll want to bring to a small venue which should enable you to cope with any eventuality. Some of these may be provided at the venue but always check before leaving anything at home.

- [ ] Projector
- [ ] Projector cables (power and connection cables)
- [ ] Spare projector bulb
- [ ] Laptop
- [ ] Laptop power cable
- [ ] International power adapters (if speaking overseas)
- [ ] Mouse and mouse mat if required
- [ ] Projector stand
- [ ] Projector screen and stand
- [ ] Remote presenter (for navigating through your slides)
- [ ] Speakers and speaker cables (if you need them)
- [ ] Your slides! (They'll already be on the laptop of course)
- [ ] Backup of your slides on an external memory device
- [ ] Something to prop up the projector
- [ ] Your handouts
- [ ] A printed copy of your presentation for your own use
- [ ] Long extension lead
- [ ] Spare batteries for any equipment that needs batteries
- [ ] Roll of gaffer tape
- [ ] Digital timer (if you have to keep your presentation to a set time)

Large venue / event

Presenting at a large venue or event should make fewer demands on you in terms of what you need to bring to the event. However, don't assume they'll have everything you need - check with the event organiser, venue or AV company to ensure that everything will be provided for you. On this note it's always worth popping the contact details of the event organiser and/or AV company into the contacts on your phone.

As with the small venue / event, you should still try to get to the venue beforehand if possible and arrive early so that you can check the setup and quickly run through your slides if there is time to do so. In terms of the projector and screen setup, this should all be done for you so you can relax and let the AV company handle all of the technical details.

When you are presenting at a large event, the organiser may ask you to send your slide presentation in advance so that it can be passed on to the AV company for them to set up. If they do, then make sure that you have clearly specified that your presentation should **NOT** be changed in any way. Yes, I've put it in bold and caps because it is such an important point. If you've taken on board what I have advised in this book then you are not going to want to put in all that effort to build an awesome slide deck only to find that the event organiser has converted your slides into their own template. All the colours and fonts have changed and the organiser's logo is suddenly appearing on all of your slides, not to mention the slide number! Specify in your terms and conditions that no changes can be made to your slides and, just in case this is ignored, take a backup of your slides on a memory device.

POP-OUT NUGGET #46

If handing your slides over to the organisers, make sure that you clearly specify that your presentation should not be changed in any way.

#46 ▶   #46

Checklist for large venue presentation

You may still want to bring various things as a backup but the checklist of things you will need when speaking at a large event is much shorter than for a small one.

- [ ] Laptop
- [ ] Laptop power cable
- [ ] International power adapters (if speaking overseas)
- [ ] Mouse and mouse mat if required
- [ ] Remote presenter (for navigating through your slides)
- [ ] Your slides! (They'll already be on the laptop of course)
- [ ] Backup of your slides on an external memory device
- [ ] Your handouts
- [ ] A printed copy of your presentation for your own use
- [ ] Spare batteries for any equipment that needs batteries

Boardroom style presentation

You may present in a room equipped with a TV or large LCD or OLED screen into which you can plug your laptop. You might be safe in assuming that, if it's a purpose-built AV facility, they will have all of the cables necessary for you to do that but, as with any other kind of venue, take along your own backup cables and adapters just in case.

Most modern screens will have one or more HDMI (High-Definition Multimedia Interface) sockets, a standard for connecting high-definition video devices. If your laptop has an HDMI socket then it's just a matter of plugging one into the other.

The advantage with HDMI is that it will carry both video and audio signals from your laptop to the screen which is important if you are using sound in your presentation.

If your laptop doesn't have the facility to connect HDMI then your best bet might still be to get an adapter that converts from the standard used on the laptop to HDMI.

Fig 33. HDMI cable and plug.

You may also be able to present wirelessly if both your device and the screen or projector you are using supports this.

If you're not sure about the size of the screen you are going to be presenting on, make sure that your slides are big and bold so that they can be read on any size screen.

Checklist for boardroom presentation

If you know the room you'll be presenting in has a screen that you'll be using, here are the things that you will need to take along:

- Connection cables (as a back-up)
- Laptop
- Laptop power cable
- International power adapters (if speaking overseas)
- Mouse and mouse mat if required
- Remote presenter (for navigating through your slides)
- Your slides! (They'll already be on the laptop of course)
- Backup of your slides on an external memory device
- Your handouts
- A printed copy of your presentation for your own use
- Long extension lead
- Spare batteries for any equipment that needs batteries
- Digital timer (if you have to keep your presentation to a set time)

Can people read your slides?

I said earlier that you should never use the phrase: "I hope that people at the back can read this slide." But how do you make sure that people can read your slides?

Well, firstly you make sure that you are using large enough text of course. If you are in an environment where you have no control over the size of the screen, this is all you can do. If you can control the size of the slides on the screen then make them as large as possible so that your slides can be read. (Although don't make it so large that your slides overwhelm people in a small room.)

Here's a useful technique that will give you an idea of the optimum size of screen for your slides.

Put your presentation into slide show mode in PowerPoint or Keynote and then move back from your screen. If, as you move back, the slides become more difficult to read then move slightly towards the screen again. Measure the distance from your eyes to the centre of the screen at which the slides are still readable and measure the width of the slide area on the screen.

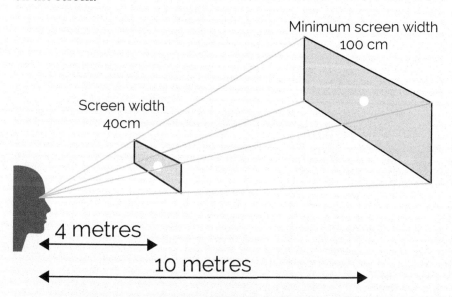

Fig 34. If you can read a 40cm screen width from 4 metres then the minimum width of your screen from a viewing distance of 10 metres will be 100cm.

If you know the length or approximate length of the room in which you'll be presenting (or more accurately, the distance from the screen to the person furthest from the screen) then you can easily work out what minimum projected slide width you'll need so that everyone in the room can read your slides. Here's the calculation:

Minimum projected slide width =

Length of room / (Comfortable viewing distance from your screen / Slide width on your screen)

Make sure you use the same units throughout for your calculation. Let's add the figures shown in the diagram to this calculation (and we'll convert everything to centimetres):

Minimum projected slide width =

1000cm / (400cm / 40cm)

This gives us a minimum projected slide width of 100cm or one metre. So you would need to make sure that your projected screen width is at least one metre wide in order for your slides to be readable.

Rehearse, rehearse, rehearse

Some people think you can over-rehearse and I agree if it means that your presentation ends up being a bit wooden. However, it's much better than being under-rehearsed, especially when you are using slides. Remember, you are putting on a show. If you're serious about using slides then they are an intrinsic and important part of that show.

POP-OUT NUGGET #47

Rehearse with your slides until you feel completely comfortable.

#47 ▶   #47

Rehearse with your slides until you feel completely comfortable. At all points of the presentation you should know what's coming next so you're not going to be caught out by an unexpected slide popping up in the middle of your presentation. This would cause you to backtrack, which will be very obvious and distracting to your audience.

You don't have to rehearse using the projector. Simply use your laptop and remote presenter to work your way through the presentation until you are completely familiar with it. You may find that you'll want to make a few tweaks to the slides or that a particular slide or build sequence doesn't quite work as well in practice as you thought it would. Better to find that out in rehearsals so you can make the necessary changes before the big day.

Rehearsing properly will also mean that you don't spend time looking at the slides on your laptop or worse still, looking back at the projector screen. A glance at the laptop to make sure you're on the right slide is all that should be needed so that you can keep eye contact with your audience.

What if it all goes wrong?

After all the effort you've put into your speech and slides, you probably don't want to think about it all going wrong. But it could, so you should!

You can't use slides

What if you can't show your slides for some reason? There's a power outage, your projector has decided to pop its clogs at the most inconvenient time or there's a software or hardware issue that you can't fix in time. Do you have a backup plan?

If you've thought about this beforehand and planned for it then you won't be floundering about at the event and wondering what to do next.

POP-OUT NUGGET #48

Plan how you can give your talk without using slides in case the worst happens.

#48 ▶   #48

Plan how you can give your talk without using slides in case the worst happens. Maybe you could distribute your handouts at the beginning of the presentation rather than at the end. Although this is a no-no when your slides are working, it may be seen by your audience as a good way of rescuing the situation when they are not.

Relying on the internet

One thing that can go wrong or be very unreliable is the internet connection. If you need an internet connection for part of your presentation then think about a backup plan in case the connection is not working or is crawling along at a snail's pace. If part of your presentation involves demonstrating some software, have screen grabs of the software to use as a backup should the internet connection let you down.

They've cut down my time

The other thing that can go awry is that the organiser tells you that, due to other speakers overrunning, your 45-minute presentation is now a 20-minute presentation. How do you cope with that? Don't be tempted to rush through your presentation as quickly as possible; that's just not going to work and won't deliver value for your audience.

Instead, your best bet is to plan beforehand what you will do if your speaking slot is truncated. Produce a backup presentation that contains slides that you can use in this instance. You could even produce two backups. It doesn't take long to do. Use the slide sorter and delete the slides and points that you think you can skip if you have less time. That way, you'll still give a polished and professional performance without having to rush.

If you are giving out handouts, these can still contain all of the points you were planning to deliver and you can explain this to the audience. Both they and the people who booked you for the talk will be greatly impressed that you were so prepared and dealt with the circumstances so proficiently.

And finally...

If you can design and build a slide presentation that engages and enthrals your audience then you will be more effective. Your message will stick in people's minds and they are more likely to take the action that you want them to take.

I've seen good, professional speakers using bad slides and that's even worse than when a poor presenter uses bad slides. At least then people will be thinking, "Oh well the whole thing was rubbish." But if you're a professional speaker, or you need to make a professional impression, then your slide deck must be professional.

Implement the hints, tips and advice I've given in this book and it will transform your slide deck from dull and lifeless bullet points to vibrant and vigorous slides.

At the end of the day, remember that it's still all about you. Your slides are not your presentation. They are there to help you RICE your talk and make it an uplifting and memorable experience for your audience!

I'd love to know how you get on with implementing the advice in this book. If you've got any feedback or you'd like to let me know how you got on with your next presentation after reading this book then drop me a line: dave@theslidepresentationman.co.uk.

It's time to go forth and wow your audience!

About the author

David Henson has worked in the digital media world ever since digital media became a thing. He started out in photography, photographic printing and analogue slide production, then he set up The Regent Slide Company in 1986 and moved into the realm of computerised graphics. Over the years it produced thousands of slides for organisations of all sizes from the company's base in central London.

He moved from slide production to website development in 1999, but since becoming involved in public speaking and, being subjected to the excruciating experience of having to sit through other people's slides, he has rediscovered the vital importance of his old expertise.

Realising that even good speakers use bad slides, he's on a mission to rid the world of boring, ineffective and unengaging slides.

He is involved in training, speaking and, of course, presentation design and production.

You can find out more on his website, where you'll also find more useful blogs and videos.

Just go to www.theslidepresentationman.co.uk

the
slide
presentation
man

The Publisher's Guide series is designed to help you make the most of the opportunities writing and publishing can offer your business. As an author or budding author, navigating the new and somewhat uncharted territory of publishing in the digital age can be a little daunting.

Most authors fail to approach their writing and publishing with a strategic perspective—this limits the potential of their projects. Every *Publisher's Guide* focuses on **developing coherent strategies** that enhance your book's quality, reach and success.

Written by Martyn Pentecost and Richard Hagen, founders of mPowr Publishing and Immersive Publishing, these guides share the insights gained over nearly sixty years of combined media experience in writing, design and editorial, publishing, marketing and presenting across a wide range of topics.

The Heist:
Cracking the Marketing Code Through Authoring a Book

978-1-907282-24-9

Storyselling Your Business

978-1-907282-59-1

Write Your Book—Grow Your Business

978-1-907282-74-4

Other Business Titles from mPowr Publishing

Mission: Leadership—Lifting the Mask
Ben Morton

978-1-907282-71-3

The Key: To Business and Personal Success
Martyn Pentecost

978-1-907282-50-8

The HR Warrior
Nicola Williamson

978-1-907282-84-3

MARKHAM PUBLIC LIBRARY

MARKHAM PUBLIC LIBRARY
16640 SO KEDZIE AVE
MARKHAM IL 60428
(708) 331-0130

CPSIA information can be obtained
at www.ICGtesting.com
Printed in the USA
LVOW06s1510151117
556395LV00021B/284/P